The Complete Guide to

CREATING & MANAGING NEW PROJECTS

for Charities & Voluntary Organisations

Alan Lawrie

DIRECTORY OF SOCIAL CHANGE

**The Complete Guide to Creating
& Managing New Projects**
for Charities & Voluntary Organisations
Alan Lawrie

Published by the Directory of Social Change,
24 Stephenson Way, London NW1 2DP,
Tel: 020 7209 5151
Fax: 020 7209 5049
e-mail: info@d-s-c.demon.co.uk
from whom further copies and a full publications list may be obtained.

The Directory of Social Change is registered charity no. 800517.

First published 1996. Reprinted 1999.

Cover design and typesetting by Linda Parker
Printed and bound by Page Bros., Norwich

British Library Cataloguing-in-Publication data
A catalogue record for this book is available from the British Library.

ISBN 1 873860 91 9

Other Directory of Social Change departments in London:
Courses and Conferences tel: 020 7209 4949
Charity Centre tel: 020 7209 1015
Research tel: 020 7209 4422
Finance tel: 020 7209 0902

Directory of Social Change Northern Office:
Federation House, Hope Street, Liverpool L1 9BW
Courses and Conferences tel: 0151 708 0117
Research tel: 0151 708 0136

Contents

Foreword

Organisations, both small and large, undertake projects each and every day. Invariably, projects are in response to an innovative idea or the emergence of new donor or client need. Idea formulation, investigation of opportunities and planning strategies are key components of any project. The voluntary sector is no exception in this. With research indicating that only one in five applications for National Lottery funding succeeds, project planning and monitoring are critical for success.

As the voluntary sector continues to grow in size and complexity, demands on the services and resources that charities and voluntary organisations provide continue to increase. NatWest has worked closely with many partners in the voluntary sector not only through our Community Investment Programme, but also through our extensive banking relationships with charities. We recognise the pressure that charities and voluntary groups are under to meet increasing demands for their services. We want to make our contribution to help the voluntary sector meet the challenges it faces and help to improve the financial effectiveness of charities and voluntary groups. NatWest's own experience has led to sound practical advice; that is why we are please to support this publication. Good luck with your project.

Sponsored by

 **NatWest**

Author's note

This book looks at all the main stages involved in turning a new idea into a viable and effective project. It is based on the experiences of many different sorts of projects within and outside of organisations. One of the main lessons I learned in writing the book was that dynamic and innovative projects rarely follow a rational and even process. People involved in creating new projects have to be skilful in juggling different demands, keeping the momentum going and bringing others on board. Tidy, organised and logical management plans and blueprints rarely work.

I am grateful to many people and organisations for helping me with this book. I am very grateful to several of the organisations that I have worked with as a consultant for letting me use their experience. Twenty five consultants, project managers and developers took part in a survey to find out good practice and learn from mistakes. Sandy Adirondack, Peter Baker, Jan Mellor and Bill Mellor offered helpful comments and advice on different parts of the drafts. I am also grateful to the Directory of Social Change for commissioning and to NatWest for supporting this project. Much of this book is based on real life case studies of successful, not so successful and disastrous project start-ups. To make the telling of the case easier and to protect the innocent, names and background details have been changed.

Alan Lawrie
September 1996

Alan Lawrie is an independent consultant and trainer who works with public sector and voluntary agencies on management, organisational and strategic development issues.

Introduction

In an average year around 9,000 new charities are registered and 115,000 new commercial companies are formed. Throughout the economy new products and services are being introduced at an increasingly fast pace. Despite uncertainties concerning future funding and future prospects there is a continual interest in creating new organisations and creating new projects.

This book looks at the key decisions and processes involved in starting up a successful new project. The book is relevant to two different types of new project:

- A project set up as an entirely new and independent organisation with its own legal status.
- A project created within an existing organisation. This could be a new service, activity or a new venture.

What is a project?

The term 'project' is often used loosely. There are several different definitions of what is and what is not a project. Here are four of the most important features:

A project is unique

There should be an idea behind a project that is new, different and innovative. It is not just a copy of what has happened before.

A project is time limited

Projects usually have a limited life. Often funding or other constraints limit their ability to become a permanent organisation.

A project creates changes

Projects should have clear plans of what they want to change. There needs to be a vision behind the project. The project should make some measurable difference. The changes should last after the project has gone.

A project is goal oriented

A new project needs to have a realistic and achievable plan and strategy if it is to make the maximum impact. The way it is managed and organised needs to be goal oriented.

Sometimes projects lack these features or they are not fully developed. Often projects have them at the start but lose them as they become more concerned about internal issues and long term survival of the project. Projects can very easily stay past their 'shelf life'.

Projects can be independent or housed in organisations. Planning them and managing them requires a different approach from many of the traditional ways in which we have run our organisations. It also needs a willingness to adapt to new ideas.

Haven't we got enough projects?

In the United Kingdom there is an abundance of charities, housing associations, statutory services, self-help groups, not-for-profit agencies and assorted quangos. In England and Wales there are over 180,000 organisations registered with the Charity Commission. So why spend time creating more new projects?

It can appear to be more effective to do something new.

Often it seems easier to start something new, either inside or outside an organisation, than to try to change what an existing organisation is doing. Most of the discussions about managing change are about doing new things. The reality is often harder. Organisational changes may fail not because people are reluctant to do something new, but because they refuse to give up the old. Many organisational changes get blocked because it seems impossible to stop doing existing things and break with the past. A new organisation or project does not have the history and traditions that can hold a new idea back.

New projects travel lighter.

Managed well, new projects can create a new identity, build relationships, operate flexibly and work faster. In an established organisation it is easy for routines, structures and a sense of 'this is how we do it here' to get in the way. A new project can have a focus and a vision that is clear and a sense of direction that can unite and excite people. In an established organisation issues of vision, values and direction often become confused. The long term survival of the organisation and the maintenance of the status quo becomes more important.

It is easier to sell a new project.

People who control resources often seem attracted to backing new projects rather than providing long-term support to existing projects. This can create a cynical atmosphere as applicants play a game with funders. Applicants automatically use words such as 'innovative' and 'creative' to repackage existing activities. Very few funders are willing to commit themselves to a long term investment. This interest in stressing the new is likely to increase as an annual total of over £1.2 billion is up for bidding from the National Lottery's five distribution boards.

There is no hard or reliable evidence about the success or failure of new projects in the not-for-profit sector. Evidence from various studies of small business suggests that as many as one in five small businesses will cease trading within two years of their being established. Market forces can easily decide their viability. Not-for-profit agencies rarely have such a severe test. Success is much harder to define. If a charity fails to meet its objectives it is likely that it will struggle to continue until at some point it will either gradually fade away or become moribund. In the public sector if a statutory project or programme does not operate as intended, action to remedy it can often be late or non-existent. It is likely that the project will be quietly forgotten. Resources will be taken away from it to use in another project. A profit test is only appropriate for a commercial company. Many not-for-profit projects lack any measurable sense of success or failure.

In researching this book the most useful evidence was anecdotal. I was unable to discover the essential ingredients that would make any new project work. No fool-proof recipe guide on how to start a successful new project is on offer. Factors like chance, serendipity, creative thinking and inspired leadership are often crucial to success. These factors are frustratingly difficult to package and replicate. It is possible, however, to describe the main tasks and processes involved and to suggest techniques and tools that can make the process of starting up an internal and external process easier to manage and hopefully creative.

Books that suggest simple formulae that can guarantee success are dangerous because many of their case studies are inclined to go through disasters and crises after publication. Today's stars often fall. Two things can be learned from this. First that success is usually only a temporary phenomenon and secondly that the critical factors which create success can often be lost along the way. However in the research and discussions for this book, eight features kept cropping up as important issues in creating and managing the successful start-up of a new project .

A clarity of purpose

There is a strong sense of vision and values. People involved in the project are focused on making a difference. They have a clear vision of what they want to achieve and the main steps towards it. Vision is the overall sense of what the project aims to do, change and achieve. It is about the big picture. Values are the ethos and principles that underpin the actions taken. Statements of vision and values need to be clear enough to unite people within the project and to explain the project to the outside world.

There is a sense of energy

Activities and work on the project have a feeling of direction and even urgency around them. People want the project to happen and are prepared to run an obstacle course to overcome barriers and hurdles in their way. The people leading the project need to be able to inspire confidence and communicate the project's vision and values.

People think objectively about the project

The people promoting the project regularly stand back and think through their assumptions about the project realistically. They ask or have to answer searching and even awkward questions such as; will it really work? is it really that new? will it make a difference? They do not let their enthusiasm for it get in the way of dealing with hard issues.

It works in an open and participative way

New people are welcome. Information is shared. Formal and informal networks of supporters, backers, friends and experts are formed to help get the project off the ground. Lots of people are encouraged to have a stake in it.

It is a team effort

Often one or two individuals have a critical role in getting the project up and running. Without them nothing happens. However, they operate as catalysts by involving and supporting other people. People at the centre of the project seem to operate as leaders and coaches rather than as sole performers, aware that few individuals have the talents, skills and patience to carry out all the tasks involved alone.

There is a flexible way of working and managing

Decision-making structures, budgets, job descriptions and organisational systems need to be clear, simple and capable of quick response to change. A tendency to create bureaucracy and to add structures and overhead costs must be kept in check. New projects need to be able to make decisions quickly, act on them and move resources flexibly. Continual change and uncertainty is accepted as the norm.

The project has a clear identity

New projects need to have an easily understandable identity and image. What it is for, what it will do (and not do) and what it values need to be presented in such a way that people can understand and pick up the central message quickly. People connected to the project should be able to describe its central ideas in headlines rather than having to write pages.

The work is exciting and challenging

Often new projects get a sense of energy from the feeling that they are being creative and that they are breaking new ground. Effective projects have an atmosphere around them and a style that is often dynamic, fast and informal. Some risks are allowed.

These features do need managing. They do not just happen. They need leadership, organisation and team work. Starting a new project is hard work and often needs determination to see it through.

It is interesting to note that the issue of finance and available resources is absent from this list. It is not that they are not important, but that they need to be seen in a proper perspective and considered at the right time. In a successful project the idea, the needs and the project vision are usually developed first. The search for cash and resources comes second. Trying to do it the other way round will often mean that the project becomes funder led. All of the ingenuity, ideas and energy behind it are suppressed to ensure that it fits the perceived interests and constraints of possible funders.

Two types of projects

One way of classifying new projects is to divide them into 'supply side' and 'demand side' projects.

A **supply side** project is one which is developed because resources are available for a particular type of project. Money becomes available (often as a result of underspending at the end of the financial year) and invitations to put forward projects are invited. The lead time in getting a project up and running has to be fast. Usually the project has to be in place by a deadline. Mistakes can easily be made as things are done quickly. In working with supply side projects some organisations have had difficulties. Often the project is finance led. No time is available to test out the project or consult with its users. At times all of the emphasis is about getting the money spent before the end of the financial year. One organisation now keeps several project outlines 'on ice'. Should resources become available, they can quickly adapt the project to fit the relevant criteria.

Demand side projects are a result of people recognising new or existing needs or gaps in provision. Often someone with a view or a sense of vision is crucial in acting as a catalyst to get people to recognise a need and generate an idea to meet it. Demand side projects usually take longer to develop. Considerable work is needed to explain the project, win support and secure backing for it. Often demand side projects struggle to get access to funding.

No logical formula

Experience suggests that the life of a project does not follow a logical and tidy path. This book is designed around six main processes and groups of tasks. They are usually not neat and tidy incremental steps. They are inclined to merge together. Management of a new project requires of all of the tasks and careful organisation of each.

Encouraging innovation.

There is little point in new projects simply copying what is already being done. It would be easier to extend or replicate what is already working rather than go through the work involved in creating a new project. However new ideas can be rare or discouraged by the way we work. Innovation and creative thinking are often in short supply. They need to be encouraged, supported and managed.

Testing the idea.

There are several different ways of testing out a new idea. Independent studies can be commissioned to research the idea's feasibility and viability. Pilots can be developed. It is also possible to simply run with the project and see if it works.

Building the case for the project.

Before a project can be launched other people will need to be involved with it and feel part of it. The essential idea and vision behind the project needs communicating and marketing. A network of alliances, backers and supporters needs to be built.

Getting the project going.

The project needs to develop a strong sense of momentum to drive it through its start-up. There must be a strong sense of teamwork. One innovator is usually not enough. The project also needs to develop a plan to guide and monitor the start-up.

Designing the project.

Projects need to be goal-centred, fast moving and able to use limited resources flexibly. Much traditional management practice and many organisational systems contradict this. Projects need to find ways of organising that support to enable them to meet their vision rather than constrain it.

Getting the project organised.

Detailed decisions about legal structures, finance and staffing will have a profound impact on the project. These issues must be planned and managed in a way that supports and enhances the project's strategy rather than restricting it.

Four factors in a successful project

Successful project management is about connecting together four different and sometimes conflicting factors:

The need for the project

Projects work best when the people developing them understand and appreciate the needs and problems they have to tackle. It is important to properly evaluate the need or problem. What is its root cause? What are the symptoms? What is the scale of it?

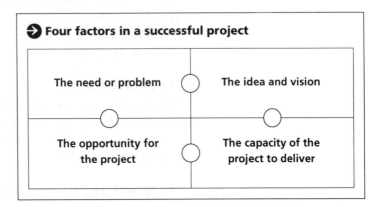

Four factors in a successful project

The need or problem

The idea and vision

The opportunity for the project

The capacity of the project to deliver

The idea behind a project

Projects need a vision to unite all their activities and efforts. It is from the vision that strategies, objectives and work plans flow. The big idea behind the project should be clear enough to show how the project will make a significant and sustainable difference to the needs or problem.

The opportunity

Projects need to have or to create the space in which to operate. Projects need to be actively supported and backed with more than just money. There must be support for the project from key people and a genuine commitment to see it through.

The capacity

Projects need the right balance of skills, energy, resources and organisation to get up and going and deliver results. Projects need to be designed so that they are able to make an impact and create results.

All of these factors need to be looked at and evaluated equally in the design of a project. Too much focus on one or two factors can lead to others being ignored. Common problems in creating new projects include:

Needs are not tested

Often projects are set up with a very hazy view of what they are aiming to address. The needs or problem are never analysed or studied properly. The project then imposes its 'solution' to a need it does not fully appreciate or understand.

The idea and vision obscures all

The individuals involved are so strongly enthused by their idea that questions such as 'Is it needed?', 'Is it wanted?' and 'Will it work?' are ignored.

The project is blocked

The project is isolated. Despite statements to the contrary the project finds little cooperation from others. There is little practical support and goodwill shown towards it. It has little space or opportunity to develop.

The project is badly designed

The project does not have the resources, people and leadership necessary to make an impact. It is top heavy. Its structures and systems inhibit it from making progress. It lacks any real strategy.

A difficult terrain – four balancing acts

New project development can be hard. Internal and external factors can easily be stacked against you. Here are four of the main issues most new project developers have to juggle with:

Insecurity and short term vision

One senior local authority manager commented that:

"Time spans have become shorter. We are under pressure to have things up and running much quicker. We need to see projects delivering much faster. Lead times have been cut. This is partly because we are often under pressure to spend money from central government and other funding programmes before a fixed deadline and also because our policy makers are increasingly impatient for change and seem to regularly change and alter priorities. For me long term planning is about eighteen months. I doubt that there are many people who could commit themselves to supporting a project financially for more than one year or two. Long term and secure funding is unlikely to happen".

This situation can easily cause insecurity and discourages long term planning. It can also create a hand to mouth existence for projects. They live from one grant application to another. Consequently any long term vision is lost or is shelved.

Security versus flexibility

At the start of a new venture it is impossible to be certain of how things will work once it is up and running. What skills will be needed? What will be the pattern of costs and income? What will be the issues that the project will deal with? It is therefore logical to resist detailed planning and to try to keep things flexible. However, funders often want to see stable and safe projects with detailed work plans and proper control systems. Staff understandably often want secure terms and conditions of employment with a detailed job description.

Managing the balance between stability and the need for flexibility and responsiveness is a difficult act in most organisations.

Fear of risk and wanting innovative solutions

In the private sector the companies that are committed to new product research and development accept that many new ideas that they invest time and money in will never make it to market. This money will never produce a return on their investment. These companies have learned to live with and indeed plan for failure. In the voluntary sector such a view is rare. Trustees are concerned about their legal responsibility as guardians of charitable money, funders express sharp concerns about wastage, managers are concerned about their credibility if projects do not succeed. However, the issue of risk and the potential for failure does need to be considered if an individual or organisation is to do anything beyond being safe, ordinary and predictable.

Balancing planning and doing

No feasibility study, market research report, cost benefit analysis or external consultancy report will guarantee that a project will work. Often it can only be properly tested by doing it. Many successful projects were never properly planned, tested or piloted. The people behind them just set them up. They worked hard at ensuring that they worked. Such talk of bold innovation and social entrepreneurship usually overlooks a host of projects that did not deliver. Project failures are often conveniently forgotten. To win resources and manage risk, promoters of new projects increasingly have to demonstrate that their idea is properly tested, is needed and has been designed. You need to decide how much time to put into testing and designing the project and when to 'grasp the nettle' and launch it.

2

Innovation – Encouraging and developing new ideas

A truly innovative idea or project sounds like a exclusive, once in a lifetime event that can only be dreamt up by talented individuals with exceptional intelligence, creativity and imagination. In reality few organisations would seriously want to manage the process of having and developing ideas in such a idealistic way. There is little direct research into how voluntary or public sector organisations develop new services or activities, even though it seems almost mandatory to claim in annual reports, funding bids and publicity material that all work is always innovative and ground breaking.

What do we mean by innovation?

There are very few new original ideas. Most successful innovations are the successful adaptation of an existing idea or the connecting together of a problem and a solution. Innovations are rarely big or huge initiatives. Innovation usually builds on what is already happening.

Many ideas happen accidentally or in the wrong place. One study by John Jewkes in his book *The Sources of Innovation* found that out of 57% of major inventions ranging from ball point pens to engineering techniques 48% were discovered whilst looking for something else, or were invented by people who should have been doing something else with their time at work.

Often innovation happens despite the official management and decision making systems in the organisation. It often happens in the shadows of the organisation. One established project working with ex-offenders developed a new and successful system of peer support and group work without ever talking to anyone at the organisation's headquarters. Four years later the scheme now employs three staff and has an expanding network of volunteers. The project leader described the process of innovation that they adopted.

"We knew that if we asked for permission to introduce the new support system it would takes ages. Papers would have to be written, reports commissioned and studies done. It would have left our hands and been taken over. Instead we went ahead with it and quietly started piloting it. Once we knew that it was working we then introduced it to

our senior managers in order to secure new funds for it. To their credit they supported it."

Many new projects are started more by chance than by organised planning. Management writer Henry Minitzberg makes an interesting distinction between **deliberate** and **emergent** strategy in organisations. A deliberate strategy is when managers clearly set out and plan how they want their organisation to develop. An emergent strategy is when things happen as a result of chance, opportunity and even accident. Many organisations have invested heavily in commissioning research, designing blueprints and detailed budgeting only to find that their best laid plans are out of date as soon as the ink is dry. Deliberate strategy is necessary. Without it total chaos would reign. However, too much deliberate strategy can make an organisation very unresponsive and inflexible.

A director of an arts centre described how she struggles to manage the relationship between these two elements.

"By the nature of our work people are having ideas all the time. Several of our workers are very capable of getting involved in something by chance or working on what interests them. On balance it pays off, but it can be a bit chaotic. Most of our established and successful activities started out as a pet project of one or two staff. If they want the idea to become a project they have to get backing for it. They have to navigate it into the formal side of the centre. They have to get a budget for it, get it programmed into our plans and get staff time to work on it. My job is to ensure a balance between the deliberate parts of the organisation (budgets, work plan, resources, business plans and contract obligations) and the emergent/ chance activities."

➜ Deliberate and emergent strategies

Deliberate strategy comes from	Emergent strategy comes from
◆ Formal plans	◆ Chance and accidents
◆ The budget	◆ People's pet projects
◆ Work plans	◆ Having the time to do something different
◆ External contracts and commitments	◆ Trying things out

Types of innovation

It is possible to identify three different types of innovation:

A new activity, service or product

Finding a new way of meeting a need is a typical innovation. The voluntary sector has a strong track record in creating, sponsoring and setting up new projects to meet new needs. Community transport, Citizens Advice Bureaux, community businesses are all examples of initiatives put together to meet a need.

A new development in practice

Many new innovations are concerned with developing different or improved ways of managing an existing problem or activity. This can include developing new processes, new techniques or using new technology.

A new strategy, direction or approach

A different type of innovation is the creation of an entirely different vision, values and direction for an organisation. This could include changing the whole basis of how an organisation works by giving greater control to users or by changing fundamentally the type of work for example. Sometimes this can only be achieved by creating a new organisation or distinct project.

➔ Just how innovative?

In 1993 Stephen Osborne of the Aston Business School carried out a research project into the meaning and extent of innovation within voluntary organisations operating in social welfare. 195 organisations from three different areas took part in a survey. This was followed up by 24 in-depth case studies of individual organisations.

The findings raise the question of the actual extent of innovation within the voluntary sector:

- 48% reported no innovative developments
- Of those that did identify some innovation 26% were of a developmental nature (the existing service is developed with the same client group) and 47% of respondents described an evolutionary innovation (where new services are provided to an existing client group).
- 15% reported expansionary innovation (using an existing service with a new client group) and 11% identified total innovation (new services meeting the needs of a new client group).
- Very few organisations claimed innovations of national significance.

The report suggests that these findings *"refute the commonplace view of voluntary organisations as all inherently innovative"*.

The follow-up case studies also found no inherent characteristic of a voluntary organisation that could predispose it towards innovative activity. Instead, the most significant factors were the expectations of key stakeholders within and without the organisation (particularly their major funders) and the ways in which it chose to respond to these.

The process of innovation

The innovative process can be described in five parts:

- Creating an atmosphere that encourages new thinking
- Encouraging creative thinking
- Exploring possible sources of new ideas
- Managing innovation within the organisation
- Developing an idea into a proposal

Creating an atmosphere that encourages new thinking

Fresh from an intensive (and expensive) residential management course, the Director of a housing association called in his staff. He told them that they had his full support to think creatively, take risks and be innovative. After his pep talk experienced members of staff remembered their last experience of innovation. A new project had failed to live up to the original expectations. Despite considerable effort and commitment from the project leader, results had been mixed and disappointing. The association had reacted by reducing the project's resources, gradually closing it down and reallocating the project leader to a boring and mundane job. The project leader was a talented and intelligent individual who had thought it was understood that some risk was involved. He was now regarded as a failure. The association gave out a mixed message: "be creative and innovative" was the public slogan, but the hidden text was "but, whatever you do... don't ever get anything less than 100% right".

Creating an atmosphere that encourages people to question the status quo, looking for better ways of doing things and come up with new ideas is not easy. A critical issue is stressing the importance of learning as a central feature of organisational life. Good learning creates an openness, inquisitiveness and curiosity which may lead to new insights and ideas. Several organisations are trying to develop the idea of a learning company which sees learning not just in a narrow sense such as attending external courses or job-related training, but also encouraging curiosity and long term development and change. Learning is seen as a main building block of the organisation.

The following ideas are examples of how we can create an atmosphere that encourages fresh thinking and innovation:

Encourage learning

Creating an organisation which encourages learning as a continual activity can lead to lots of new ideas. Learning does not just occur on training courses or in seminars. Effective learning can be organised in many different ways; mentors, secondments, distance learning, coaching and guided reading are all examples of ways in which it can occur within the workplace.

One housing association is experimenting with the idea of giving each member of staff a minimum of five days' learning entitlement per year. They can use this time to attend formal courses, but many are now using it to evaluate existing services and develop ideas for new ones.

Encourage evaluation

Building in regular evaluation activities can be a way of encouraging new ideas. Evaluation techniques include surveys, review meetings, audits and discussion groups. Building regular evaluation into all aspects of the organisation's work can encourage innovation.

An arts centre now holds a review conference after each event.

It has two parts to it. A 'post mortem' discussion looking at what worked and what did not and a 'what next' session to look at what has been learned and to generate ideas for the future.

Encourage curiosity

Often in organisations working practices and processes fall into a routine. Things happen because they have always happened. The budget and the work plan are based on what happened last year. The organisation operates on 'automatic pilot'.

Encouraging people to ask why we do things is important and often challenging. Getting an organisation focused on the results and impact of its work rather than the volume of it can be one way of encouraging fresh thinking.

Encourage feedback

Developing new means of generating comments, reactions and complaints from the organisation's users, staff and other contacts can lead to several insights. Formal systems such as complaint procedures, satisfaction and review sheets are part of the process but are no substitute for 'walking the job' and being able to observe and listen to people.

Often even negative feedback, such as a complaint can highlight the way in which an activity can be improved, changed or enhanced.

Encourage flexibility

People need to see the wider context and effect of what they are doing. Where jobs and work are compartmentalised, few people see the whole picture. Through flexible working, job shadowing and job enlargement people see much more of the whole picture.

An architects' practice changed how they managed projects. Staff were encouraged to manage a project through from start to finish and indeed to regularly visit it after its hand over. This small change (often called job enlargement) led to several improvements and better coordination of projects.

Encourage movement

Often people get stuck in a particular job. Their perspective of and involvement in their work becomes narrow. They lose a sense of vision and purpose. Some organisations are encouraging staff to move round different projects, to become multi-skilled and to use appraisals and review meetings to chart their progress. Well planned and supported movements can help to encourage an exchange of ideas and views.

Manage conflict

Often conflict is seen as wholly negative and to be discouraged at all costs. However, well managed conflict which is focused on the problem and not the personalities involved can spark off many insights and ideas. Getting different parties to a conflict to work together to define the issue, explore root causes and generate possible ways forward could provide new and valuable ideas.

Experiment with structures

New ways of working such as secondments, project or task groups and team work can lead to creative solutions. The structures should help people to look at things from a different point of view and develop new ideas.

A national development agency has used project teams extensively over the past two years to develop key projects. Four or five staff from different functions work together for a short period on an issue and come up with a plan. Often the people with the least prior experience of the issue make the most valuable contribution. Their asking of obvious (or seemingly idiotic) questions challenges conventional practice and assumptions.

Get away from it all

Often you can be too close to a problem to think about it creatively. One company found that staff returning after short breaks, sabbaticals or transfers came back with a different insight to a long term problem.

One charity for people with learning difficulties holds an annual ideas day. All staff, board members and volunteers meet off site and are required to bring at least three new ideas to work on. The day works through each idea and develops a short-list of ideas to implement on return.

Borrow from others

Some organisations have got the process of stealing from others off to a fine art. Keeping in touch with developments in your field through professional bodies, networks and conferences is important. One project organises what it calls raiding parties where staff visit similar organisations to look at how they do things and see what could be adapted in their project.

Encouraging and supporting creative thinking

Most ideas do not come from staring aimlessly at a blank sheet of paper in the hope that, like a flash of light, a new idea will burst forward. They are more likely to come from a development of what you are already doing. We need to improve our skills to see the space for and ingredients of a new idea.

Creative thinking techniques

Creative thinking can be learned and improved like any skill. Various techniques and models can be used to free up our thinking and encourage creativity.

Common blocks to creative thinking include:

◆ A tendency to conform
◆ Fear of risk and failure
◆ Failure to challenge conventions or assumptions
◆ Polarising alternatives and choices
◆ Fear of looking foolish
◆ Working to rigid drawn boundaries

Some of the most common creative thinking techniques are:

Brainstorming

Brainstorming is a well established tool. It works on the basis that from a wild or unusual idea something that is practical, creative and useful will emerge. There are three simple rules to brainstorming:

1. A problem or question is posed.
2. As many possible ideas are generated and recorded by the group.
3. All ideas are reviewed and possible solutions built on.

In the second stage it is important to go for as many ideas as possible. Participants should be encouraged to think freely and say whatever comes to mind. No criticism or discussion of anyone's idea should be allowed at this stage. All ideas should be recorded on a common list so that in the third stage no one feels obliged to defend or justify their idea.

Lateral thinking

Edward de Bono developed the idea of looking at a problem both logically and laterally. Logical thinking follows a rational plan; the problem is defined, information is gathered, formal criteria for solving it agreed, options discussed and the most efficient option selected. Logical thinking is useful and helpful. However it can be restrictive and lead to solutions that are predictable and unexciting.

Lateral thinking is different. It places a much greater stress on challenging the problem, challenging any assumptions in the way that the problem is posed and trying to turn the problem upside down. The central idea behind lateral thinking is to avoid moving

---

Will it work?

"Heavier than air flying machines are impossible."
Lord Kelvin, President, Royal Society, 1895.

"Everything that can be invented has been invented."
Charles H Duell, Commissioner, United States Office of Patents, 1899.

"We don't like their sound, and guitar music is on the way out."
Decca Recording Co. rejecting the Beatles, 1962.

directly from problem to solution. Instead it encourages you to search for an answer by looking at the situation differently. For example a problem might not be a problem at all. A threat can at the same time be an opportunity. A strength can also be a weakness. Typical lateral thinking questions are:

- How can we look at this problem differently?
- How is it connected to other issues?
- What really is the problem?
- What is the root cause of the problem and what are the symptoms?
- How could the problem be turned into a solution?

Lateral thinking encourages you to think differently about the problem.

Six hat thinking

Edward de Bono also went on to develop a six thinking hats technique. His idea was that all individuals and groups can get stuck into a particular approach to a looking at a problem. Good individuals and groups should be able to wear all six hats in looking at an issue.

White hat thinking

Deals in facts, known information. White is objective, neutral and unbiased. White is only interested in sharing information and establishing facts.

Red hat thinking

The red hat is about feelings. It allows expressions of fear, excitement, passion, personal taste and intuition. It encourages hunches and 'gut reactions'.

Yellow hat thinking

The yellow hat is all about being positive, constructive and about making something work. It looks for the positive.

Green hat thinking

This hat is all about being creative and encouraging the growth of new ideas, options and alternatives. It is concerned with fresh thinking.

Blue hat thinking

Blue hat thinking encourages structures, logic and organisation in problem solving. Blue hat thinking focuses on tidy and managed processes and decisions.

Black hat thinking

The black hat thinking plays the devil's advocate. Black hat thinkers look for problems, risks and pitfalls.

Exploring possible sources of new ideas

New ideas can be developed in many different places. Here are four ways in which new ideas can be discovered:

A fresh look at what you are already doing

This can happen either through formal processes such as commissioning an evaluation of what you do, carrying out surveys or comparing it to others in the same field. It can also happen accidentally. One environmental agency developed an entirely new way of working with schoolchildren as a result of some challenging questions asked by a newly appointed clerical worker. She thought that the way the schools programme was organised was out of date and unimaginative. After asking several 'awkward but painfully obvious questions' she persuaded the rest of the team to work with her to develop a new and very different project.

Challenging the way that you look at a problem

Often we get stuck into a predictable and routine way of thinking about a problem. We do not challenge or rethink our assumptions or ever look at the difference between the root causes and the symptoms of the problem. Trying to see an issue from a different perspective, thinking laterally rather than just logically, or testing the validity of assumptions about the problem can all lead to a creative solution. Often we jump to solutions without first checking that we fully appreciate the problem and all of its aspects.

A voluntary agency had debated for years what to do with its overcrowded and increasingly expensive city centre office. Various solutions were debated such as moving, changing the office layout and building an extension. A session on creative thinking led to a different solution. At least half the staff were supposed to be working on neighbourhood projects and did not need to be office based. The office was only ever overcrowded between 10.00 and 16.00 and it was particularly overcrowded when field staff had to attend meetings, use the computers and attend supervision sessions. The agreed solution was that the central office needed to be smaller, with two satellite sub bases rented near to where the neighbourhood workers worked. Meetings and supervision sessions would be held at the sub bases. Field workers would be given laptop computers and be able to e-mail material to and from the main office. This solution created significant benefits. It reduced travel costs, reduced stress at the central office and, most importantly, refocused the organisation by shifting the physical presence to the local neighbourhoods from the city centre. By looking at the problem differently it discovered a useful and fruitful solution.

Adapting a solution from elsewhere to a new problem

Many innovations occur when something can be adapted from one use to another. All it requires is the capacity to make a connection between a need and a link to a possible solution elsewhere. Much of the technology we use in our households started out life in industrial, commercial or specialist fields. For example, the TV remote control was originally designed as a niche specialist product for people with disabilities. It was not seen as having much mainstream potential.

Following up an opportunity

Many established organisations lack a capacity to identify new needs and encourage feedback from users. The organisation is inward looking. It operates to a very narrow menu of what it can provide and offer. A severe example of this was the manager of a local authority service who complained that members of the public kept phoning up his staff and *"asking for the wrong things"*. Organisations may define themselves so tightly that opportunities are dismissed as not relevant.

Often people working in a particular sector or field make sense of it by developing their own language, practice and style. This is understandable, but can lead to a very narrow focus, with staff able to relate only to people who speak the same language.

Often narrow thinking leads to a compartmental approach to thinking. Our starting point is what we do now and not what is needed. Creative thinking requires us to move away from our usual way of looking at or describing something. We need to learn and innovate from what we already do. We need to develop a broader understanding of what is happening in the world outside and be willing to be flexible as to how we can respond. Opportunities can be missed if people are too busy dealing with day to day issues.

Most organisations do what

● CASE STUDY

Thinking and operating narrowly

A sports development project decided not to bid to a specification for a contract with their local health authority to develop a healthy lifestyles campaign. They felt that the project specification did not 'sound like us', although the actual work involved and the anticipated outputs and outcomes were almost identical to what they were currently doing. The specification was written in a health professional's language rather than a sports development one.

they are doing now as a result of history. They are driven by what they did last year. Keeping going and ensuring that existing expectations and commitments are met is often enough. The internal routine takes over. The main driving force is survival and ensuring that things continue from one month to another. The organisation develops an atmosphere in which it is too busy to think, plan and respond to new opportunities.

Managing innovation within the organisation

Managing an organisation that genuinely supports and encourages innovation is hard. It involves undoing a whole way of operating and managing that has developed over time. But for innovation to happen within an organisation this process is necessary. The alternative is for managers to pay lip service to creating new activities, but become frustrated as little happens.

Project development cycle time

In certain industries (in particular the car and computer industries) considerable effort has been made to cut down the time it takes to develop, design and produce a new product. The time involved in product development is known as the 'time to market'. New models of cars can now be designed, tested, engineered and produced in three to four years as opposed to the seven years it used to take. Many companies believe that their competitive edge will increasingly come from being first to the market with new and innovative products and services. Organisations have invested heavily in streamlining new product development systems, in creating much more effective internal processes and in rewarding successful individuals and teams. Few not-for-profit agencies have the resources available to invest internally or reward success in financial terms. But it is interesting to look to see what (if any) internal process manages the development of new projects.

In one well established organisation a brief review was carried out. The review was prompted by the comments of one individual that *"it took so long to get an idea agreed that it was not worth bothering with, as by the time approval was given it would be too late".*

Three projects were used as case studies. Development time (the time from having the idea to the project being launched) ranged from nine months for a media campaign to three years for a local project. Despite innovation being one of the main buzz words of its new mission statements, very little actually happened. New ideas had to run an obstacle course of meetings, reviews, planning sessions, budget cycles and detailed considerations. Many ideas got lost on the way. If it did get through, it was a wonder that there was anything left in the idea at the end of the process.

The review indicated four problems which frustrated new developments and suggested how they could be tackled.

No time

The organisation operated at full capacity. Few individuals had time to think and discuss new ideas. The working style was all about being seen to be busy.

Action: Responsibility for developing new ideas would have to be seen as an explicit part of managing the organisation. Work plans, job descriptions, budgets and meeting agendas should have 'development' built into them.

No process

People sponsoring a new idea had to navigate it through a plethora of meetings and committees. Responsibility for making a decision to back an idea was often avoided or put off. 'New ideas often hung around waiting for a green light.'

Action: Responsibility for managing the process of project development and approval should be given to a senior person within the agency. The number of stages involved in getting project approval should be cut.

The present comes first

Many people assumed that there was never any money for new ideas - so why bother having them! The main planning activity in the organisation was the annual budget. It should be the clearest statement of priorities. The starting point for putting the budget together was first to cost in expenditure for current activities and projects. There was hardly ever any surplus income for new work. Yet many of the items in the budget were no longer priorities. They were there because of past decisions rather than current strategy.

Action: The organisation should review all of its activities and projects periodically and see how they fit with current direction and needs. Budgets for new projects should be considered at the same time as existing projects and activities.

No resources

The organisation did not have any financial resources to invest in new projects. Funders were perceived to be unwilling to allow them to develop any reserves.

Action: The organisation should build up a development fund equivalent to 4% of its revenue. This fund should be used to support, test and 'pump prime' new projects. The rationale behind this fund should be argued for in the business plan as a sound management idea.

There is an emerging opinion amongst several observers that larger organisations find doing new things much harder than smaller ones. In the private sector large conglomerates such as ICI and IBM have redesigned themselves into smaller units, encouraged decentralisation and task forces to get away from the notion that intelligent thinking and effective management are only the province of the corporate headquarters. New ideas can get lost in office politics, demarcation battles and numerous committees and meetings.

One senior manager in a large national charity described how he is trying to turn the organisation around:

"We are working hard to break down the barriers between our head office and local projects. We are reducing the number of things that need to come to us for approval, we are encouraging our project leaders to keep some time back for exploring local needs and planning new projects. We have created a small development budget to work on new ideas or to allow for staff cover to do project development work. We want to turn around the view that all ideas must come from the top. It has not been easy and will take a while to work properly".

Organisational structures and practices can easily, but unintentionally, discourage people from having or taking forward new ideas. Many organisations operate at or even beyond full capacity. Every hour is in demand and all income is tightly allocated to existing commitments. Most of our structures and practices are about controlling what is already happening rather than allowing space to develop new projects. Tight job descriptions mark off boundaries and can sometimes stop people seeing the whole picture. Narrowly written funding contracts and business plans mean that every ounce of resource is committed to existing projects and service delivery. A lack of any uncommitted money or working capital means that opportunities to develop new and worthwhile activities are missed.

Lost opportunities

There is an accounting term called 'opportunity cost'. An opportunity cost is when an organisation has committed itself so much or is using all its existing resources to the extent that it is not able to follow up or invest in a new opportunity that emerges.

An opportunity cost happens when one decision or activity stops you from being able to do or follow up something else. For example, a contract with a local authority might be so demanding that it leaves you with no time to develop other projects, make contact with other purchasers or bid for other work. The opportunity cost of the local authority contract is the cost that you forego by not having the management time to develop other work and create other income.

Often we incur opportunity costs by being too busy and not having any uncommitted time or money to explore and test new ideas. The cost of being busy is losing the opportunity to develop and innovate. An organisation risks becoming inward looking. Opportunities are often ignored because we become so involved in what we are doing that we fail to keep in touch with new developments and ideas. It is important to commit time to finding out new developments and spotting possible opportunities. A director of a voluntary agency described how he does this:

"I have a rule that I spend at least one day a month away from the agency, at conferences, visits to similar projects or with our main user groups. We are a well established and generally successful organisation. But I get concerned about being complacent and failing to develop. I push people to keep in touch with the outside world. It encourages us to question what we do and helps us to identify options and opportunities for development".

Developing an idea into a proposal that can be considered further

The final stage in innovation is often the most tricky. It involves persuading other people that there is a basis of a sound idea which should be considered further. The initial enthusiasm, creativeness and even excitement of the people who support the idea may well clash with the caution of those who need to know that the idea is viable, feasible and relevant.

The next chapter looks at different approaches to testing an idea's feasibility. There is a stage before that which is to convince other people that the idea for a new project should be explored further.

It is easy to come up with reasons and objections as to why something will not work, why a new project is flawed and even why the people proposing it are naive and not fully experienced. It is harder to achieve a balance between encouraging innovation and a realistic appraisal of the idea.

Four factors are useful in the process of deciding to progress a new idea:

Focus the discussion on the big picture

The discussion should be on the need for the project, its possible benefits and how it could work. Factors such as detailed costings, who will fund it and who will staff it are probably unknown at this stage and should not dominate the discussion.

➲ Start at the end innovation

One interesting technique in developing a vision for a new project is to start at the end and work backwards from it. This technique is commonly used in developing new technologies. The marketing departments of some computer companies have even been known to announce the intended launch of a new product before the product has been fully designed. Innovators sketch out how you would like things to be, look and operate. Questions of how will it work, how much will it cost and how will it happen are suspended.

Once the end scenario is clear, work can begin on identifying how to overcome gaps between where we are now and where we want to be. It has three main advantages:

❶ It produces a very clear vision of what you want to achieve

❷ It is future oriented. Its starting point is where you want to be rather than the problems and issues of the present

❸ It gives a very clear goal by which progress can be measured

It also helps to make a distinction between 'ends' and 'means'. Ends are what you hope to achieve, make different or change. Means are the methods, activities and services we use to get there. For example an advice service could make the following lists:

Ends	Means
◆ People better informed about their rights	◆ Accessible advice sessions
◆ Combating poverty	◆ Recruiting and training volunteer advice workers
◆ Highlighting the need for effective measures to tackle poverty	◆ Specialist legal services Social policy campaigning Telephone advice lines

Often we spend too much time looking at the means to such an extent that the ends get lost or become vague. Sometimes we get involved in means that do not take us towards an end. In recent years the term 'outputs' has been used to describe the means and the term 'outcomes' to describe the ends.

Stress the vision

Spend time on why the project is needed. Do not assume that people understand the context, specific situation and need for a new initiative. Often people presenting a new project have laboured on it for so long or are so enthusiastic about it that they fail to outline the need for it and the background to it.

Acknowledge uncertainties and unknown details

People introducing an idea at this stage can often disarm potential objections by drawing attention to things that need testing or further consideration. It is useful also to indicate possible risks rather than let people spot them. They should seek agreement to consider it further and not seek a complete agreement for immediate implementation.

Actively seek allies

A new project needs backing early on. A useful way of doing this is to listen to and acknowledge the ideas, reactions and suggestions of others. The project may well fail if it seen as being an individual's pet project or hobby horse. Use people as sounding boards and ask them to add to your idea rather than find fault with it.

➡ 21 statements designed to kill a new idea

It is easy to reject a new idea. Often organisations develop a style that encourages instant rejection or discouragement of new ideas. Some of the reasons may well be valid. Others may not be:

1 Excellent idea... let's set a committee to study it further

2 It needs considerable research

3 We are too busy with day to day work to go into it further

4 Why don't you write a detailed paper and come back in three months' time

5 There's no money in the budget for new ideas

6 They tried it at XYZ agency and it didn't work

7 How do you know that it will still work in five years' time?

8 Interesting idea but let's talk about the details

9 If you produce a five year budget forecast and a five year cash flow projection, we will consider it further

10 Personally I think it is a good idea, but ... won't like it

11 Please ensure that everyone is consulted about it and happy with it before we discuss it further

12 Funders won't like it

13 It doesn't fit with our five year business plan

14 Let's remember to include it in our next five year plan

15 There could be risks involved

16 We will only move on it when every possible problem has been considered and worked through

17 We only do new projects when we have guaranteed permanent funding

18 This is just a passing fad... I have seen it all before

19 Good idea, why don't you start on it straight away alongside all your other work?

20 We tried something similar five years ago and it didn't work

21 Isn't that a new idea?

Testing the idea

Once you have decided that you have an idea that is worth pursuing there are three ways forward.

- You could carry out a feasibility study to check that there is a real need for the project and to check that the project will be able to make an impact on the need.
- You could pilot the project on a smaller scale for a fixed time to see if it does work.
- You choose to skip feasibility studies and pilot projects and simply go ahead and do it.

The third choice may seem reckless and extreme. However it is worth remembering that many effective projects and ideas would probably have failed a feasibility study.

When to skip a feasibility study

When time is short

Delaying the project while you do a feasibility study will only lose time. It is more important to do something rather than wait.

When you can live with it failing

When you have sufficient confidence and security to live with failure if it goes wrong. You are able to cope with the risks involved in the project failing.

When you can minimise risk

The project is designed to be flexible enough so that it can adapt itself to what works and stop what does not work. It must be able to change course or be able to be closed down painlessly if it clearly is not working.

Making the decision on how to test your idea will be determined by a number of factors:

- The likely attitude of potential funders for the project
- Your attitude to risk
- Time and other resources available to test the idea

It is alleged that scientists at Farnborough carried out a laboratory research exercise into the aerodynamics of the bumblebee and concluded that it would never be able to fly. In many ways the only true test of a project is to try it out. Feasibility tests, pilot projects and market research are important, but cannot guarantee success or failure.

The factors that make a successful project are varied. They include many human and one off factors such as goodwill, luck and local circumstances. Many feasibility studies can be criticised for only dealing with objective information in an illogical world. There is a tendency to consider only hard facts and ignore information such as reactions, opinions and comments that need more interpretation.

However, to avoid waste, to convince funders and to check on our original plans, all ideas for projects need some kind of study to show that the idea is sound and worthy of investment. Increasingly, clear evidence is required to show that a new project could deliver results, is needed and is worth the investment.

What to test?

Six questions can form the basis of a new project's viability test:

- ◆ Is it really needed?
- ◆ Does it fit with other projects/activities?
- ◆ Will it attract sufficient resources?
- ◆ Is there a body of support for it?
- ◆ Are the expected results realistic and worth the effort?
- ◆ Does it fit with what we want to do?

Is it really needed?

All projects should be aimed at meeting a need and making some kind of sustainable difference. But the history of voluntary and public sector projects includes several examples where a community's needs were ignored or a need was confusingly identified. Five things can go wrong:

Confusing needs and wants

Often discussion about what people need is passive, general and is influenced strongly by what the people commissioning the study want to hear. This often happens when an established organisation decides to consult with its current or potential users. The discussion is usually constrained by boundaries of the existing services and activities. What a person wants can be a different matter. It is more about personal choice, aspirations and preferences. It might be ambitious to focus on wants rather than needs but often it leads to a much more creative and effective project.

A self help agency consulted at length with the intended users of a new project. The results of the needs survey indicated that of the suggested services, day care and counselling were the most needed. Six months later the project was set up. Attendance at the day centre and take up of the counselling service were very poor. A casual conversation with two potential users indicated a likely reason. The needs survey was general and impersonal. They had answered the questions by thinking about what they thought 'average' users would want. They personally would not want to attend a day centre or use counselling but at the time it seemed sensible to suggest that others would need them.

Only dealing with the surface problems

A useful approach to needs analysis is to recognise that a problem may have different layers and only some are immediately obvious. For example, problems of juvenile street crime will probably have a range of symptoms, problems and root causes. Lack of leisure facilities, youth unemployment, dysfunctional home life, inadequate policing, poor public safety and a lack of alternative role models are just some dimensions to this type of problem. It is easy to tackle only one or two dimensions of a problem (often the ones that you are most experienced in or interested in) and ignore deeper or more complex aspects of it.

Often researchers are so interested in finding a solution that they do not spend sufficient time analysing the problem and challenging how it is presented.

Being fixed on the solution

Often a study is commissioned and carried out with a solution very clearly in mind. The problem is shaped to fit the solution. In one inner city area a respected community activist described what happens:

"We have had numerous vocational training programmes provided by central government. The courses have been good, but have not led to the economic regeneration that is needed. Indeed some local people are now on their third or fourth course. Training is important but it needs to go alongside job creation, small business support, child care, transport on and off the estate and basic educational skills. However, all the recent research work has only looked at training and not looked at the whole picture".

Not really listening

Occasionally there is a tokenistic or cynical approach to research and consultation. It is done in order to produce credibility and evidence to win funding. The overt or inherent assumption is that the research will find nothing which would challenge the assumptions behind the intended project. The project is already designed; all that is needed is some evidence that it is wanted.

Coping rather than changing

A useful test in designing a project is to think about the overall vision behind the project. What kind of sustainable impact will it make? Will it really change things or will it merely make things more tolerable for a short term? Will the ideas behind the project make a real difference or will they only make a superficial change for a short period?

What depth of intervention is needed? Is it better to do a few things that will create real change rather than spread resources widely and limit your impact to coping better?

Does it fit with other projects/activities?

A new project needs to be tested against existing or likely alternatives. Commercial organisations expect designers of new products to highlight their 'unique selling proposition'. A USP is what your project can do or deliver that others do not. A similar process needs to be adapted to test out the fit between a possible new project and its environment. Two different questions are worth asking:

Who else is doing similar or related work?

A useful technique is to map out all other agencies doing similar or related things to what you want to do. It is important when mapping other agencies, individuals, organisations and companies involved in the project's sphere to think broadly. One or two comparisons will usually be obvious, but others may be identified after some time.

Can the sector or market support a new project?

What is the size of the market for the project? Is it cluttered with other projects competing for funds and clients? Is there clear space for a new project? What are the main trends in the sector or market? Is it likely that demand for the project will increase, stand still or decline?

It is also useful to compare the proposed project with existing or likely alternatives.
- What will be different about your project?
- What will it offer that will be distinctive?

Possible answers might point to what it does and what it delivers or how it works or its relationships to its users? You need to be clear how you will measure the difference. Often the distinctive difference is more about how you do something rather than what you do.

- Will its impact be greater or more distinctive?
- What will your project do that others do not?
- Will its impact be more relevant?
- Will it be more effective?
- Why will it work better?

If the project is unlikely to be much different or its impact similar to or the same as existing projects then the question of why bother to start out must be raised. Why set up a new project if all it will do is what others are already doing?

Will it attract sufficient resources?

At the start of any new project this question is often uppermost in people's thinking. Increasingly no certain answer is possible. Short term funding programmes, changing priorities, political and economic uncertainty all make any long term confidence about funding impossible. Conversely this issue can be ignored by the promise or guarantee of initial funds for the first year or so (often with no guarantee of future funds). Three things are worth looking at:

Is the financial basis of the project sound?

Detailed costing at this stage is very difficult, but it should be possible to estimate the main costs involved in starting up and running the project. Are there particular aspects of your project where costs are likely to be unusually high or difficult to control?

What assumptions can be made about likely income sources?

The accuracy of the information you collect here needs to be evaluated. You need to balance optimism and realism. Some projects do not get off the ground because they are unable to prove without a shadow of a doubt that they will attract funding. Others are backed at this stage on the basis of vague promises of funding from unnamed backers. It is worthwhile collecting three types of information:

Indications of definite or highly probable income. It may be that funders have indicated that they will back the project and provide funding or contracts. Unconditional promises are usually hard to find and difficult to get on paper.

Feedback from potential funders. Informal soundings from potential backers can be very helpful. The idea of the project, but

● CASE STUDY

A sustainable proposal?

For six months a specialist advice agency had informal discussions with the secretary of a charitable foundation about a possible new piece of work. The foundation indicated that they were interested in funding a pilot project around the issue of small business debt. They wanted the agency to submit a proposal. They wanted the project to demonstrate what could be done rather than simply research need.

The foundation has made it very clear that they were only interested in funding a project for at the very most 18 months. They wanted to stimulate new ideas and encourage mainstream funders to take up new work. They would not consider funding on going commitments.

The grant would have paid for the wages of at least one and a half specialist workers and provided a management fee in recognition of the costs involved in running the project. Other obvious funders said that they were interested in the scheme, but held out no real possibility of providing any new long term funding.

When the possibility was discussed at a management committee there was a wide range of views expressed. Everyone recognised the need. It was noted that small business debt was a highly complex and drawn out area – many cases could take years to resolve. Three broad schools of thought emerged:

❶ Ignore the deadline. With luck something will turn up. All funding is good.

❷ Run it but be prepared to end it if necessary. Try to get other funders involved.

❸ Redesign and renegotiate it so that it can start and end within eighteen months.

The discussion highlighted several critical issues in project design and development relating to risk, sustainability and the need for strategic thinking. The agency decided to proceed with the project only if the funder would agree to an action research project into small business debt. The foundation rejected this and the project did not take place. The agency's manager commented that

"It was probably one of the hardest decisions we have ever made. To turn down funding runs contrary to the way that many voluntary organisations operate. But, from an organisational and service point of view it would have been irresponsible to have gone ahead with it".

not the detail of it, should be market tested. Possible funders or purchasers should be approached to comment on how the project would fit with their priorities. Do they recognise the need? Could they ever envisage backing it?

Evidence of acceptability for statutory income. The project may need to conform to relevant legislative or other standards if it is to access statutory income. Increasingly projects operate in a regulatory environment in which in order to operate or receive payment, clear standards have to be met. Child care, residential care and legal aid services are all examples of this. Meeting these standards will have time, cost and staffing implications. Unless the standards can be met it is unlikely that the project will receive income.

Attention also needs to be given to the medium term indications of funding. This may involve some realistic assessment of the stability of current income sources and the likely capacity to develop new income sources.

What about non-financial resources?

Is the project dependent on volunteers, resources given in kind or other hidden income? How safe are these inputs? What would happen to the project's costs if they were withdrawn or declined? One project was set up operating in a office donated by a local church and dependent on a team of volunteers. Such support was taken for granted when the steering committee first discussed it. The appointment of a new vicar led to the project becoming homeless within its first few months. This led to the volunteers drifting away and no new volunteers being recruited. In a few months it went from being a promising project to a disaster. It had been set up 'on the cheap'. It had no contingency plans or thought for what could go wrong. It had assumed that goodwill would continue.

Is there a body of support for it?

A simple test is to map out what level of support there is for the project within different groups. Possible groups might include:

- Direct users
- Supporters
- Decision makers
- People indirectly affected by it

There needs to be a 'critical mass' of people who demonstrate a sense of ownership of and commitment to the project. They need to be prepared to invest their own time and effort into the project and be willing to fight for it. This can be a difficult issue to assess.

A steering group set up to develop an environmental project was well attended and seemed to have the basis of a strong core group. It met together for nearly a year. The idea behind the group came from one person who had brought together all of the steering group. She did all the organising work, drafted the project's plan and marketed the project to others. Very little was delegated to other members of the group. When she was ill for three weeks nothing happened. The planned steering group meeting went ahead, but was embarrassing. No one knew what was happening, no one even knew what needed discussing. What it revealed was that the vision and concept of the project was only held by one person. It was felt that to set up a project on that basis was flawed and would create a very vulnerable project. For the project to move forward the original innovator had to do less. Others had to be involved not just as a supporting cast but as key players.

Are the expected results realistic and worth the effort?

A rough balance sheet needs to be drawn up to assess if the work involved in setting up and running the project is likely to be paid back by the benefits generated.

A traditional approach to this would be a value for money study. This involves testing the anticipated results against the criteria of:

Economy	Are the costs involved fair? Could it be done cheaper?
Efficiency	If it were organised better could we do more? Are the results worth the costs?
Effectiveness	Will it create real lasting benefit?

Such an approach depends on sufficient information being available. You also need to be able to make a fair comparison to other projects and have a clear sense of what value the project is trying to create.

An alternative and less financially driven approach is to realistically predict what difference the project will make in terms of what it creates and what it produces (**the outputs**) and what difference it will make for the users and society as a whole (**the outcomes**).

Such predictions need to be carefully discussed and explored. The accuracy of any assumptions about what can be achieved and what can be sustained need to be evaluated.

It is important to test if the project really will make a difference. Often projects are set up without a sense of what impact they will make. A project to introduce arts to isolated rural communities

● CASE STUDY

A project for changing things or marginal improvement?

In May 1994 two Indian Community workers Stan and Mari Thekaekara spent a month in Britain looking at how poverty was being tackled in three areas. Their first impression was "so many organisations and such a lot of resources, but why so little impact or change?". They looked at how organisations identified needs and intervened and recorded the following observation:

"The moment a problem is perceived, concerned individuals or organisations immediately concentrate their energies on trying to raise the necessary funds to tackle that particular problem. Translated this means writing up a proposal then hunting round for somebody to fund it and finally setting up a project to deliver a service that addresses the particular problem of a particular group of people. And very often this service was of the highest order. But this does not lead to the eradication of poverty. It makes life more bearable for the concerned people. But the fear, the low esteem, the marginalisation - all remain".

A fuller account of their visit can be found in another DSC book, **Across the Geographical Divide***, see page 135 for further details.*

concentrated all of its efforts on reaching as many people as it could. They felt that the issue of access was important to them and contact with high numbers would impress funders. The project's plan for the first two years would mean that people in each of the local communities would only get three to four two-hour sessions with the project. The actual value of this was questionable. Apart from a brief introduction to a new art form what real skills or insights could be developed? The benefits of the project were not obvious or sustainable.

Does it fit with what we want to do?

It is possible that an idea for a new project is sound, viable and sustainable but not the right one for an existing organisation to set up. Three issues are relevant:

Legal and constitutional fit

The activities involved in a new project could take the organisation outside of its remit. The aims and objectives clause and the intended area of benefits may restrict the organisation from taking it on. For example a charity's constitution may restrict it from operating outside a particular geographic area or only with a particular client group. It may decide that it does not wish to alter its governing documents in order to do so.

Synergy

At some point all the activities involved in an organisation need to connect. They need to create a whole picture. If they do not the organisation will become fragmented and lack purpose. New projects need to fit with other activities. A director of a development agency commented:

"Three years ago we went through a dreadful phase. We stopped being a united organisation and became a loose collection of projects that had little relationship to each other. Some were very practical, some experimental, others were about policy and research. We lost our identity".

How broadly or how narrowly you seek synergy between projects may need to be discussed.

Skills and management fit

It may be that an existing organisation does not have the right balance of skills to manage it. It may lack the structures to house it. If an existing organisation is not able to support or direct the project properly then the chance of the project's success will be limited.

If it is felt that the project is a good idea, but in the wrong organisation, then options such as encouraging an independent project or transferring the idea to a more appropriate organisation should be considered.

Carrying out a feasibility study

Feasibility studies vary enormously in terms of scope, content and style. Some are the product of detailed independent research carried out to a strict methodology. Others are much more open-ended and deal more in people's opinions and impressions.

Types of studies

The six questions listed at the start of this chapter provide a broad overview of the types of issues a feasibility study could explore, but detailed examination of all of them would in most cases be very time consuming, expensive and unwieldy. In broad terms there are three main types of study. The type of study needs to be agreed at the outset.

> **Outline structure of a feasibility study**

Introduction
Brief details as to how the study was commissioned. Who carried it out? When was it carried out?

Background to the study
Why was the study carried out? Is its purpose to identify needs, check that a project would work or test the market for it?

Assumptions before the study
A summary of the main assumptions that the people who commissioned the study want testing. Examples of assumptions might include 'the belief that a particular need is not being met' or that 'no other organisation is doing anything similar' or that 'this project could be self financing'.

Issues that were tested
List the specific questions that need answering in as concise a way as possible so that it can be seen later if the study has met the original needs.

Methodology
When and how the study was carried out. The different techniques used to gather information and the organisations and people who were contacted during the study.

Findings of the study
The findings should be presented with as little commentary as is possible. Thought should be given to how statistical information can best be shown and also how opinions and reactions can best be presented.

Observations from the study
The study team should be able to outline their main observations and any interpretation that they might have of any findings. They should be able to comment on any issues that may not have been part of the original brief but may have come to light during the study. Such side issues are often very useful.

How the study can inform the development of the plan
The findings need to be matched against any existing or proposed plan. In this section attention needs to be given to how the lessons from the study can be applied to any future project.

Main conclusions and recommendations
The main conclusions should summarise the study and draw from it any specific recommendations for future action.

Needs based

This type of study is focused much more on the need or problem identified than the proposed solution. It usually involves establishing exactly what problems exist, their size and extent, and testing how different solutions might overcome them. An example of this might be assessing the causes of family break up in an area and from this research identifying the need for a family centre open at weekends.

Consultative

This type of study is about 'testing the water' for a project. Usually it is clear when the study is commissioned what sort of project is intended or is being actively considered. The aim of the study is to check that the project would be welcome, establish how best to organise and launch it and to see how it can best fit in with other agencies. For example, a steering group of people concerned with legal rights might carry out a feasibility study to determine how best a law centre could operate in their city, what should be its priorities and how should it work alongside other advice agencies. The results of the plan will be used to shape their thinking as they develop their idea into a proposal.

Market based

This type of study is often commissioned when the idea of the project is at an advanced stage. Its objective is to test out with potential funders, users or customers the details of how it will operate. Its focus is on the detailed logistics and management of how it will operate. A new arts venue might commission such a study to assess anticipated audience levels, ticket prices and programme details. The findings of the study will play an important part in building up the centre's first business plan.

Designing a feasibility study

In designing a feasibility study three main focuses can be used to develop specific questions:

Which of our assumptions about our idea need testing?

Often the most fundamental assumptions are never checked or explicitly stated. Assumptions to check include:

- Is there a real need for what we want to do?
- Is there really support for what we want to do?
- Do other people share our values and concerns?

It is useful to list what information and data you will need to consider the project further and work up a plan. Information needs could include:

◆ Current details of needs and local circumstances
◆ Mapping other provision or similar activities
◆ Available resources and their criteria
◆ Feedback we need from other people about our idea.

Questions in this area relate more to people's reaction to the project. Possible issues here include:

◆ Positive and negative reactions to the plan
◆ Potential support, rivalry and opposition
◆ Advice and ideas for the project.

Who should do it

A feasibility study can be carried out by people already involved in, people new to it or a combination of both. People involved in the project already may be able to design and draw up a study and carry it out. It will be important that they are able to think about and describe the project objectively and not see the study as a way of selling it.

Several external people and institutions undertake feasibility studies. Universities and colleges, consultancy practices and freelance consultants will all offer some expertise. It is important to shop around and find out about particular strengths and past experience. When working with both internal and external people, the terms of reference for the study should be clearly agreed and recorded from the start. They should list the areas you want studied, the specific questions that you need answering and the timetable for the exercise.

One organisation successfully used a combination of internal and external people to carry out a feasibility study on a planned new project. A small steering group of staff and committee members was set up to work alongside an experienced consultant. The consultant helped to clarify the areas to test and designed the methodology. Interviews and consultations were carried out by three placement students and volunteers. Their results were collated and analysed by the consultant. The steering group studied the findings and prepared a final report.

Gathering information

Good feasibility studies are able to deal with different types of information. A useful way of grouping different types of information is by way of 'hard' and 'soft' information. Hard information includes statistical data and factual information, such as census returns, relevant rules and regulations and quantitative survey returns. In developing a new project good and relevant information is needed to:

- Check the accuracy of our understanding about needs and problems
- Show evidence of the need for the project.

Gathering information can be a long and exhausting task. There are particular dangers involved in over-using some sources of information or not fully interpreting the findings. There is also a danger of over-using hard information (statistics and data) and ignoring soft information (opinions and reactions) sources.

Primary and secondary research

Primary research is information gathering and study of an issue or a need which has not been investigated before. You might choose to commission or carry out some primary research into an issue or need which you believe to be unexplored or to need looking at with a different insight. True primary research is unique and should have a line of enquiry which is unexplored. **Secondary research** is carried out by collecting together, reviewing and interpreting evidence, data and findings which have been researched and published by other parties.

Primary research methods include:

- Questionnaires
- Postal surveys
- Telephone surveys
- Interviews
- Group discussions
- Case reviews

Before commissioning original research, be sure it really is original. There's no point in duplicating someone else's work. One way of finding out is to contact information officers in relevant organisations or to ask an experienced librarian to check research directories.

If you decide to commission original research, make sure you know what you want and why. Research is all-too-often commissioned because nobody knows what else to do with an idea or a project proposal. Be clear about your needs. Research is not worth doing unless it's done well - and that can cost money, especially if it is original enquiry.

In quantitative research, sample sizes often have to be high to get statistically valid results. Get advice from professional

→ Information sources

The following are examples of some of the most common sources of information on needs and trends:

Index of Local Conditions (Department of Environment). The index measures relative levels of needs across English local authority areas. It provides a useful summary of data for each local authority area drawn from census and from employment, health and education sources.

Annual Abstract of Statistics (Office for National Statistics). The latest economic, financial and social figures, drawn together from monthly and annual statistical publications.

Eurostat. Basic statistics of the European Community (HMSO). Includes data on population and social conditions, economy, services and transport and the environment.

General Household Survey (Office for National Statistics). The current edition is based on interviews with about 18,000 adults carried out between April 1993 and March 1994. The General Household Survey annual report series provides valuable data on people, families, households, burglaries, health and disability, employment, pensions, education, sport and leisure activities and housing.

Population Trends (Office for National Statistics). Quarterly journal of statistics on population, childbirth, marriage, divorce, migration, death, abortion and statistics summaries.

Regional Trends (Office for National Statistics). Official statistics about the regions of the UK. Social, demographic and economic topics are covered. A wide range of data from employment statistics to infant mortality, house prices to agricultural investment is included.

Social Trends (Office for National Statistics). An annual review of British life. Well presented sections on employment to leisure, education to health, transport to housing.

Other sources of secondary information include:

Local statutory authorities. Local authorities, health authorities and quasi statutory bodies such as Training and Enterprise Councils (TECs) usually have a research and information section which should be able to advise on local issues. Published documents such as community care plans, children service plans or annual reports from health authorities should contain relevant information.

Other organisations. Other projects may well have published or unpublished information in the shape of reports, service plans, user profiles and needs analysis.

researchers before you start - it may cost, but you could save money in the long run. Secondary research involves finding useful and relevant sources of information which can be used to test out needs and ideas. There are many sources of published research. Careful thought needs to be given to their appropriateness to the project which you are developing.

Using the information

It is very easy to intentionally or unintentionally distort or misuse information. Changing the format of a graph can create a significantly different impression. Comparing one set of statistics with another may seem reasonable but may not be a relevant or fair fit.

The following points need to be kept in mind when using statistical information:

- Often surveys gather information over such a wide area that they report on broad trends rather than specific needs.
- The time involved in designing a methodology, carrying out research, collating data and interpreting findings can be lengthy. Sometimes information arrives far too late for it to be useful.
- Often to make the research process and findings manageable, information has to be aggregated together. This makes real interpretation hard. Often the research raises as many questions as it answers.

Good information gathering should use a mixture of **hard information** gathered by primary and secondary research and **soft information**, i.e. the gathering of non-quantitative factors such as feedback, opinions and preferences.

Soft information is information that is usually not able to be reduced to numbers. This could include people's emotional reaction to your idea, their personal preferences or opinions and odd bits of history, past experience or prejudice.

The balance between the two is interesting. Nowadays no computer manufacturer would launch a new system without taking into account factors such as 'user friendliness' or the quality of design or appearance. Yet ten years ago many computer manufacturers only concentrated on technical performance and capacity. The growth of the personal computer market was driven as much if not more by soft factors such as user friendliness and accessibility. Getting the balance between hard and soft issues is now critical in determining the success of a product in the market. The project might be cost effective, logical, well organised and well planned,

---

● CASE STUDY

Using a focus group

Testing an idea need not be a major task that involves huge surveys and questionnaires. One commonly used marketing technique is run a focus group. Facilitators run a short discussion group with potential consumers and purchasers. The group only needs to have five or six members and meets only once or twice. The facilitator outlines the idea to be tested, works through a list of structured questions and then encourages a discussion.

One estate improvement project used this technique by running six separate focus groups for children, young people, single people, parents, elderly people and for other agencies working on the estate. Two independent consultants acted as group leader and recorder. Each session started by a brief presentation of different options for estate improvement.

The project director was very pleased with the results. *"We got much more useful information from the groups than we would have got from a survey. A lot of the most useful feedback was about people's preferences and informal opinions that a questionnaire cannot pick up. Many of the casual comments made about what would and would not work were the most useful ones. The groups were a conversation rather than a one way exercise. We intend to use different focus group throughout the project to monitor reaction."*

---

but for it to work there needs to be a feeling of enthusiasm, goodwill and energy.

Effective studies use a methodology that can pick up hard and soft information and ensure that it can be presented usefully.

Using the study's findings

The study's findings must be fed back quickly. There is little point in delaying since the basis of the findings is likely to change quickly. The document or report is only a part of the feasibility study. People who worked on the study should also be able to talk about their impressions and assessment of the information presented.

The conclusions need to be talked through to see how far they change the original idea or outline of the project. There needs to be a degree of discipline and objectivity in how this is done. Quite often when presented with findings that challenge the original idea, over-enthusiastic and passionate innovators respond by questioning the methodology or validity of the study. They shoot the messenger.

A well-designed feasibility study can provide valuable background to the decision to proceed, but cannot guarantee success or make the decision to go ahead with it for you.

Running a pilot project

A pilot project is a scaled down version of the intended project, aiming at doing one or all of the following:
- Field test the project to see if it works in practice.
- Run it to see what successful features can be passed onto other projects and identify weaknesses that need solving before moving onto a bigger scale.

◆ Interest potential backers and supporters by showing a scaled down project in action. This is sometimes called a 'demonstration project'.

A project can be scaled down in several ways. It can operate in a narrower geographic area, or it can work with fewer people or it can limit itself in scope or remit.

Pilot projects need to be designed well. Thought needs to be given as to how long a pilot has to run in order to draw conclusions. It is difficult to design the pilot in such a way that it will be an accurate study in micro of the real thing. The following points should be built into the design of any pilot:

Make sure that pilot can fail as well as succeed

Often we learn more from things going wrong or not working out as intended. Pilot projects need to be encouraged to be experimental and seen as a learning process. The reality is often different. Often the pressure is on to get it right first time and be totally successful. Staff employed on a pilot often pick up a message that if it works it will become permanent and will provide them with secure work. There is sometimes a belief that funders need to see a perfect working pilot before they commit themselves. These factors can hide learning, discourage experimentation and distort reality.

Make sure that the pilot is as real as possible

One national agency set up a pilot to demonstrate a strategy to involve young people in their communities. The eighteen months pilot was a major success. It worked well, obtained a high profile, enthused people and prompted four neighbouring local authorities to agree to fund a project in their local area. The four local projects did not work out as anticipated. Results were low. Huge amounts of time had to be spent fundraising and gaining access to key people rather than doing the work. One project was closed early. One probable reason for this was that the pilot received such a high profile and interest that was impossible to replicate into the mainstream projects. The attention of external evaluators, visitors from other authorities, media interest all encouraged people to make it work. For the pilot, doors were opened, money found and resources provided. The four mainstream projects were unable to command this degree of attention.

Build in review points

It is important that learning and evaluation points are built into pilots. A variety of techniques such as diaries, review meetings, users panels, external evaluations and interviews can be used to identify progress. They can help us to find out what works and why and, most importantly, help any projects that follow to learn from the pilot's experience.

Making the decision to go ahead with the project

Many projects just happen. No one ever really gave approval to them to go ahead. People just start them off and only talk to others about them when they need to (usually to get money). This is not a totally disastrous state of affairs. It can produce creative and imaginative projects. But it can also produce chaos and disorganisation. At worst, projects that fail can threaten the credibility or viability of the rest of the organisation.

The decision making process needs to be carefully thought through. The right people will need to be involved. People with organisational responsibility (Trustees, Directors and managers) and people with a significant stake in the project (staff, users and possibly funders) may need to be involved. They will need to have the right level of background information. They will all need to operate to the same criteria. People involved in the early development of the project will need to be able to enthuse people to back it and at the same time be realistic about potential problems or unknown elements. Several techniques exist to help this process which is sometimes called project appraisal.

Cost benefit analysis

In this technique, the known costs of the project are matched against the anticipated benefits. The costs need to take into account all costs not just financial ones. These include time, equipment, management support and other resources as well as organisational costs such as the cost of it not working and the cost of not being able to follow up other opportunities. In compiling the analysis, different weighting can be given to factors.

Risks analysis

All activity involves risk. The following five risks are common in many projects:

- **Financial risk:** Costs could escalate or income not materialise.
- **Legal risk:** If the project does not work properly the organisation or individual trustees could face liabilities.
- **Credibility risk:** If the project fails the organisation's name and credibility could be damaged.

● CASE STUDY

Using a cost benefit study

A cost benefit study looks at all the potential costs and anticipated benefits from a project. It should look at all costs and benefits – not just financial – and also at short and longer term factors. It is a useful tool for summarising complex information and helping people reach a decision.

Costs and benefits

A national agency carried out a cost benefit study of creating a publishing unit to produce a limited number of publications and books. The study summarised all known costs and likely benefits.

Costs	Benefits
Start-up costs of £10,000	Our membership provides an instant base market for most publications
Break even point will be in year 2 or year 3 – we would have to underwrite this venture for at least two years	We have a unique position in the market. No other publisher has our expertise or connections in this market
Price of each publication will have to be at least £10 to cover cost	Publications are an effective way of informing and disseminating our work – this would support our agreed strategic direction
Publishing is a volatile business. Costs and market trends can change quickly	In three years time we anticipate this venture being self-financing and possibly creating a small income source
Will need a part time staff post in year 1	Publications will raise our profile. They will create broader interest, enhance public interest and media coverage

Analysis of the study can be built on by adding a points weighting to each factor:

3 points for very significant factors

2 points for significant factors

1 point for other factors

- **User risk**: If the project does not perform properly it could set back, harm or damage our users.
- **Delivery risk:** The output of the project is not certain or within our control. We depend on other people or factors.

The project can then be evaluated under each of these risks. Likely risks are evaluated and action taken to minimise the risk.

Attitudes to risk

We need to look at our attitude to risk. There are two extreme positions: an unrestrained and reckless attitude that ignores risks in the pursuit of the goal, or a punctilious and cautious attitude that only feels safe with a project in which every possible risk has been reduced. Both approaches are ineffective.

One strategy is to use a 'waterline' technique. New projects can be developed as we think best provided they do not endanger the parent organisation sponsoring the new organisation. The 'waterline' is the integrity, core values, financial balances and profile of the organisation.

Worst case scenario

A worst case scenario is an exercise in which pictures are drawn of what are the worst things that could happen to the project and what would be the effect and implications of them. Possible scenarios might include funding ceasing, key people leaving, drastic increase in competition and other such crises. Worst case scenarios are a useful way of assessing risks and identifying what safety nets are needed to protect the project.

➲ A risk analysis matrix

This matrix is a simple way of judging the risks involved in a project. It compares the level of anticipated risks in a project against the anticipated results.

There are four steps in using the exercise:

❶ Decide the project you want to test

❷ Ask if it faces high risks or low risks

❸ Ask if the results are likely to be low, medium or high

❹ Use this information to allocate your project to one of the four boxes

Anticipated risks	Anticipated results	
	Low/medium results	Medium/high results
High risks	**Box 1** Are the results worth the risks?	**Box 2** How can we protect ourselves against the risks?
Low risks	**Box 3** Is it worth doing?	**Box 4** Do it!

Possible risks are:
◆ Financial risks
◆ Legal risks
◆ Credibility risks
◆ Risks to the user

Possible results are:
◆ Volume of services and activity
◆ Impact and outcomes
◆ Financial returns

Box 1 projects (high risk and low medium results) should be reviewed to see if they are really worth bothering with. The level of risk outweighs the anticipated results.

Box 2 projects (high risk and medium/high results) may well be attractive given some kind of safety net or contingency plan. Can the risk be reduced, shared, protected against or insured?

Box 3 projects (low risk and low/medium results) may lack any sense of challenge or innovation. Are they worth the effort?

Box 4 projects (low risk and medium/high results) providing the assessments of anticipated returns and results are accurate look well worth backing.

Support for the project

The main objective at this stage is to build up sufficient support from people and organisations whose involvement will be critical. The time involved can vary from a matter of weeks to a year or more. It needs to be carefully monitored with progress evaluated and tasks reviewed.

Creating a steering group

A small group of committed people is probably of more use than a larger group with differing levels of interest in and commitment to the idea behind the project. The group needs to have the time to devote to setting-up, running and building support for the project. It may well be that this group will go on to become the project's first management committee, trustees or board.

A good steering group needs the right balance of relevant knowledge, contacts, expertise in funding and organisational management. All members of the group need commitment to the project's vision and values. It may be possible to have people seconded to the group to develop the project or to use a consultant to aid the process.

The group needs to be task oriented, concerned about progress and able to build up enthusiasm for the project. It should not be seen as yet another committee or meeting to attend. Setting a time limit to the steering group stage often works well. If the group cannot get the project moving in say nine months then the whole idea may need to be reconsidered.

Producing a project outline

A project outline can have three main uses:

- The discipline of writing it can help the promoters to clarify their ideas and ensure that they have a unity of purpose.
- It can help to involve others. Targeted circulation of the outline to potential partners, backers and decision makers, asking for their comments and interest can be an effective way to build a network of support.
- It can encourage people to contribute to the detailed design stage. Their comments on the outline may well be valuable in designing

the project. The more people are involved in the early stages, the more chance there is that they will be supportive later.

A good project outline needs to convey the following:

The overall vision and values of the project

The project outline needs to set out in simple terms the 'big picture'. It needs to communicate what the project hopes to achieve, why it is important and the benefits that can be expected. It should also highlight the core values or philosophy that underpins the project.

Evidence of needs

The need for the project should be set out by summarising relevant facts and evidence. This should be kept brief, but should be localised as much as is possible. It may also be useful to link the needs into any statutory responsibilities or indicate how the project will work alongside other organisations.

Evidence that the project's ideas have been tested and could work

Evidence of past work, your track record, experience of running similar projects and results of any feasibility studies should be summarised to indicate that the project is realistic and has been tested. It might also be useful to indicate if the project is part of a wider organisation and how the organisation adds expertise, support and value to it.

Short outline of how the project will work and what resources it will need

A brief description should be made of how you envisage the project working, its location, its staffing and outline financial plans. This need only be a basic sketch of how you expect to fund the project.

The document should be short. Two or three well designed pages should be sufficient to convey the main ideas. Its purpose is to stimulate interest and discussion. The style of the document should be sharp, active and realistic. Make sure that its objectives are achievable. It's worth keeping in mind the old marketing maxim, 'under commit and over deliver'.

Drawing up a project's success criteria

A very practical technique in developing a project is to draw up a project success criteria. The technique centres on the question 'At the end of it, how will we know that the project has been a success?' It has three main benefits:

◆ It focuses the mind. People developing the project need to think clearly about what will be the real impact of the project. What will be sustainable?

◆ It can also help to agree a realistic vision for the project. It is a positive tool. Often in not-for-profit agencies words like 'success' are not used enough. The tool gives people working on the project something to aim at.

◆ It aids planning. Once the success criteria have been agreed, planning can start by linking up where you want to get to with where you are now.

● CASE STUDY

An example of project success criteria

A small project set up to improve and develop the skills of voluntary management committees drew up the following success criteria for its two year project:

Hard criteria

◆ Between 400 and 600 trustees trained in their role and legal responsibilities.

◆ A core training programme, resource bank and other material capable of being passed on to other network agencies will be in place at the project's end.

◆ Between 2 and 4 management support networks will have been established and will be able to carry on meeting without external support.

◆ At least 6 consultations will have been carried out with local groups and that main learning points of these studies will have been disseminated.

◆ Funds and resources secured to ensure that trustee training will continue to be available in some form locally.

◆ A network of individuals and organisations able to demonstrate good practice and provide training and support to other groups will be in place.

Soft criteria

◆ A measurable improvement in the quality of governance and management within the local voluntary sector.

◆ Fewer conflicts within agencies as a result of disagreements over roles and relationships.

◆ Increased awareness of the importance of good management practice and good governance in local agencies.

◆ The management of this project will itself be an example of good practice that others can learn from.

Different kinds of success

It is best to keep the success criteria brief. Writing it in headlines on one side of paper is much more useful than having lots of detailed criteria. It is very important to include a mixture of hard criteria (things that are easy to measure by counting) and soft criteria (things that usually require some kind of judgement).

Hard elements

◆ Keeping to target deadlines
◆ Balancing the budget
◆ The volume of output is in line with the project plan
◆ The project is reliable and well run
◆ The project created measureable added value
◆ Activities and other projects will follow on from this project

Soft elements

◆ Keeping stakeholders committed to the project throughout
◆ The project causes minimal disruption
◆ The output meets agreed quality measures
◆ The project operates in line with our ethos and values
◆ We learn from this project
◆ The experience of the project is disseminated to others and influences their work

Building a network of support

A common tactical error is to see the development of support and external contacts solely in terms of getting cash. Funding usually follows only after a relationship has been built, common interest established and confidence in the project's sponsors established. The objectives for this stage are to identify and make contact with people who may back the project now or in the future.

A useful technique is to map the different people or organisations who are important to the project or have influence on its success. They may include:

◆ Intended users and people connected to them
◆ Sources of income
◆ Supporters/ volunteers
◆ Decision makers
◆ Regulators
◆ Relevant communities
◆ Potential partners and allies

It is possible to map out your current relationship to them and their investment or interest in the project. From this it is useful to

● CASE STUDY

Mapping support

The steering group of a new project aimed to provide an alternative to custody for young offenders. Young people would work with the project to develop driving and vehicle maintenance skills as well as broader social education. They drew up a map of the relationships they had and needed to have. At the centre they placed the project. Where they positioned each contact or interest represented the current state of the relationship. A short line between the project and the contact represented a close relationship. A long line represented a distant one. Where no contact or relationship with the project existed a dotted line was drawn.

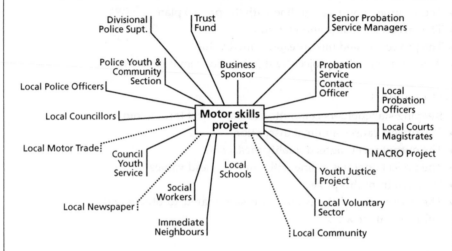

This mapping exercise highlighted three major issues for the project:

❶ The project had little direct contact with key policy makers such as senior probation service managers and local councillors. The project had a fairly good relationship with front line workers, but not with people who made decisions. The steering group drew up a list of individuals to talk to about the project and hopefully to win their support.

❷ There were several people such as the immediate neighbours, the local newspaper and the local motor trade who had the potential to take a hostile attitude to the project. The project agreed to produce some positive publicity material explaining the idea behind their work and run two open days for the public.

❸ There were several people who worked in similar fields who would be important to the project. Some would be crucial in making sure that the project got referrals, others could feel that the project was stepping onto their ground and competing for funds. The group agreed to establish a project advisory group of interested professionals to ensure that it complemented existing provision.

develop a strategy to market the project and develop a useful relationship.

A community development project has used this technique on several occasions. Their development manager described how they work:

"As we develop a project in a new area we make up a list of all the people who are or should be significant to us. We spend time visiting them, explaining the project and asking for comments. We look at how we can overcome potential problems or correct misconceptions. I think that it is important to be open with people about our plans and be prepared to listen. Time spent building relationships early on always pays off".

It is worth looking in the map for potential conflicts and tensions. For example, a new project opening a hostel in a residential area may be able to predict some prejudice or anxiety from local neighbours. It needs to develop a strategy to manage this and create an effective relationship or at the very least minimise damage.

Building a financing strategy

Questions about who will pay for the project often crop up far too early. They block creativity and innovation. They are dealt with before the project's idea has been properly thought through. The cloth is cut to fit the price. It is important that the project outline is worked out before issues of financing are addressed.

The next chapter will go on to look at the detail of costing a project. At this stage it is important to explore the different types of income available, to draw up an outline cost structure and to develop a strategy to ensure income.

Balancing different types of income

Getting money for your project takes up an increasing amount of time. Policies, criteria and practices change regularly. In many instances the term 'funding' is becoming out of date. It is being replaced by contracts and agreements. The relationship is changing from one of grant giver and grant receiver to one based on carrying out a defined piece of work in return for a fee. Often an investment or a partnership relationship is preferred to the historic one of benevolent funder and worthy supplicant.

Balancing income is also harder. Many sources of income are becoming increasingly targeted and are reluctant to fund what has been traditionally called 'core costs' such as administration and management. Some income may be restricted or earmarked so that it can only be spent in an agreed way.

● CASE STUDY

Thinking strategically about funding

Hashmere Skills Centre appointed a new director. The centre managed four projects connected to economic and community development. In his first few weeks the new director realised that the way the centre raised money was at best confused and at worst chaotic. Three particular problems were evident:

❶ Often projects were under costed

❷ Enormous effort went into chasing tiny amounts of money

❸ The centre did not manage its relations with the people who funded its work

He persuaded the management board to set up a team of three to review and develop a strategy for funding future projects. They reviewed previous projects, looked at how projects had been costed and interviewed representatives from their main funding bodies. Their recommendations were sharp:

One of the centre's main income sources was the Training and Enterprise Council. The TEC staff knew very little about what the centre did; they rarely visited the centre and only received formal monitoring information about the statistical performance of projects. The relationship with several of the centre's backers was confused and out of date. The centre used terms such as 'fund raising', 'grant aid contribution' and referred to them as 'funders'. The various bodies who supported the centre's projects wanted a much more active relationship than simply 'putting up the money'. They wanted a partnership centred on developing joint initiatives, sharing ideas and know-how and learning from each other. One programme manager commented that all he had from the centre was requests for money.

The centre's backers needed to know, (and the centre ought to know) what a project would cost. They were not interested in making a financial contribution to the centre's overall running costs in the hope that it would trickle down into projects. Their budget should sponsor projects relevant to their objectives, with a 'reasonable amount' paid as a management fee to the centre.

The management board recognised that this would require a different approach. They would have to spend more time getting and keeping project backers. Over six months the centre took three main initiatives:

♦ It implemented a marketing plan whereby key individuals from current and potential backers were invited to the centre and encouraged to see themselves as investors in its success.

♦ Potential backers were consulted at the ideas stage of a project, not just asked to fund projects. Their reactions and advice were welcomed.

♦ A newsletter for partners was developed giving quarterly information on developments, progress reports and success stories. It was circulated widely in partner agencies, and not just to their named contact officers. Its objective was to raise the profile of the project.

The centre has moved away from a traditional budget and adopted a cost centre framework where each project is a centre. All costs are allocated to or shared out amongst the cost centres. For the first time the full cost of running a project is known. The full cost of some fund raising was also clear for the first time. The centre director can point to early results of this plan. *"We do have a much closer relationship with our sponsors. We are now being invited to work with them in a much more collaborative way which is leading to some new (and properly resourced) projects."*

There are four main sources of income:

Statutory sources. Traditionally central and local government have grant aided projects to provide support. This relationship is in a state of flux. Several local authorities and health authorities have moved into a contractual relationship with voluntary organisations. Central government programmes such as the Single Regeneration Budget (SRB) increasingly regard voluntary projects as being part of the network that delivers their programme rather than a 'good cause to fund'. Open ended grants where the public authority agrees to fund a project without stipulating what strings will be attached are few and far between for new projects.

Trust and foundations. The vast range of charitable trust, corporate funding and other foundations operate very differently. Some are quite secretive in their affairs and operate mainly through personal contact and recommendation. Others have clear criteria and processes for awarding grants. In this category, (although practically a category on its own) sits the National Lottery. The five distribution boards are transforming the opportunities available to fund new projects.

Public fundraising. The different methods of raising money from known supporters and the public at large are well-documented and are expanding continually. Public fundraising in its various guises has become much more competitive and consequently expensive. Shifting trends in giving and changing public opinion make reliance on regular public fundraising an unlikely option for many projects.

Earned income. Provided voluntary organisations keep within their charitable objectives the capacity to earn income through selling services exists. This can take the form of charging for activities through rent income, fees, charges and trading. Projects which plan to rely heavily on earned income should first test the market, understand how it works and be able to make informed judgements about how they will operate within the market.

In estimating income three balancing acts may need to be performed:

Statutory versus voluntary. A difficult ethical issue is how to define what activities should be regarded as statutory functions that the central or local state should provide directly or under contract and what activities should be met through voluntary or charitable purposes. To what extent, if at all, should a project use resources provided by supporters and charitable income to support, complement or enhance services which we might expect to be statutory? For many agencies this has been a tricky line to draw.

Short term and long term income. Few sources of income offer projects the safe prospect of long term guaranteed funding upon which to build long term sustainable activities. Short term funding can be hazardous. Several projects have been delighted by the interest and backing they attract when they are new only to find that interest is not there even two years down the road. Often being 'new' is a convincing reason why projects attract income. A project needs to weigh up the risks involved in starting up without strong indications of longterm funding or it must design its organisation so that it can be scaled down or closed without harm.

Earmarked and non-restricted funds. Often projects are started as a result of money becoming available that can only be spent on a particular activity. Examples of this might include statutory sources that restrict expenditure by criteria of geography, client group or activity, or income from fundraising where the donor has granted it on the express understanding that it can only be spent on a particular activity. The relationship between restricted and non-restricted funds is a tricky one. Over- reliance on restricted funds can mean that the project becomes distorted. It is rich only in some parts.

The coordinator of a health project described how restricted funds caused problems for his new project.

"Over 45% of our income for the first two years came from a health authority contract for work with young people. This money was tightly monitored by the authority who insisted that it could only be spent on work with young people. This caused two problems for us. First, the issues we worked on were not particular to young people, but we had to bend the way we described and monitored our work to fit the contract's restriction. Secondly, the health authority were reluctant to allow for more than 7% of the fee to go on project management costs. This caused us major problems when costing for other activities. Other projects had to contribute much more towards admin. costs. In effect they subsidised the management costs of our work with young people."

An outline cost structure

At this stage you need to work out in broad terms how much the project will cost. This does need not be a detailed exercise, but you will need outline figures to discuss with potential backers. Detailed costing techniques are discussed later in this book, but it is important not to under estimate the outline cost of the project. Promises made here that the project will operate on a low cost are inclined to come back and haunt you later.

A funding strategy

Fundraising is now an industry. Consultancies and professional fundraisers are keen to offer (for a fee) advice, information and expertise. However, it is important that devising a funding strategy for the project is a mainstream consideration rather than something which is abdicated to a fundraiser.

The funding strategy needs to be informed by the project outline, the project business plan, the anticipated balance of income sources for the project and the outline cost structure of the project. Lots of organisations waste time in fundraising by not having any clear sense of strategy and become driven by being busy rather than being effective. The following are the basis of an effective strategy:

Research and test first

Do not judge your fundraising work by the volume of activity that you undertake. Lots of fundraising effort is worthy but wasted. The level of work involved does not merit the return. It is important to spend time researching the possible income sources available, finding out about relevant criteria and practice and deciding how best to make an approach. One national project employed a consultant to develop their funding strategy by testing the project on six possible local authority purchasers in field visits. In arranging the visits the consultant made it clear that she wanted advice and guidance rather than cash. In return the agency received some very useful feedback and advice which it used in designing its approaches to authorities.

Design a project marketing strategy

The term marketing often confuses people. It is often wrongly seen as being entirely about selling. Effective marketing is different. It is about four elements:

- Understanding how the market for the project operates. How are decisions about resources made? How do other players in the market operate? What is the economic position of the market? Is spending likely to go up or down?
- Determining how the project can best fit in the market. What will the project do differently? Where should it focus its resources?
- Deciding how best to enter the market. How can it best be launched? Who are the key opinion formers? What would persuade and influence them to work with you?
- Deciding how best to stay in the market. What do we need to do to keep and improve our position?

● CASE STUDY

A market survey

A voluntary organisation decided to develop a home support project to work with clients in their own homes. The service would be paid for by individual unit contracts for each client from the local Social Services Department (SSD). It carried out the following market audit. The survey was carried out by talking to key people and asking their advice on how the project could best be developed.

Information	Marketing issues
How does the market operate?	
Client assessed by Social Worker	We would have to be on approved list. We meet
Social Worker picks service provider from	criteria
approved list and district office arranges contract	We would need good contacts and profile with
Service monitored by SSD	local SSD managers
SSD have 'rate for the job' of £7.25 per hour	
Some potential for user to purchase extras	We would need high volume contracts to
SSD reviews prices annually	break even
Some flexibility for isolated clients	We should prepare costed menus of extra services
SSD has reputation for slow and erratic payment	We need to build in contingency for cash flow
Some private companies claim to operate at £5	We could offer SSD a slightly reduced unit price for
per hour	the guarantee of block volume purchase
SSD is under very tight budget constraints	
How can we best fit?	
SSD has had problems with two private companies	We must stress our quality assurance and training
Anxiety about poor quality and poor training of	programmes
staff	Launch pilot in the East Division
SSD has had difficulty getting services in the East	
Division	
How best to enter the market?	
Central contracts team manage approved list	Prepare approved list application
Assistant director willing to consider block	Present business plan, quality assurance system to
purchase	SSD
28 local area managers control spend budgets	Mail, visit and develop personal contacts with local
	managers
	Ask to speak at team meetings
	Invite SSD to participate in our training sessions
Deciding how best to stay in the market?	
SSD becoming interested in quality management	Explore cost and benefits of quality management
User feedback very important to SSD	system
SSD recognise that there are some specialist needs	Develop client feedback system & satisfaction audit
which this service may not meet	Keep some time aside for developing innovative
	services

Build interest and relationships first

All too often new projects use a cold calling approach. They ask direct for funding without building relationships. A key part of the marketing strategy should be how to inform interest and involve potential backers. This might include testing your ideas on potential backers, asking for help, involving them in consultation on the project's outline and listening carefully to how the project can best work with them.

Recognise lead times

In most instances the time involved in introducing the project, developing interest, processing a funding application and getting a decision is under estimated. In the public sector the budget setting process is practically an all year round activity. A new project has to win support from officers, win political backing, identify where funds can be taken from, go through a several stage priority bidding process and then be approved in a formal process. Early involvement and an understanding of the stages involved makes good sense.

Make links

Few backers are now prepared to give money away without expecting some kind of direct or indirect connection. The funding strategy needs to identify what kinds of mutual interest or need the project can satisfy. Possible interests may include advancing a policy or social interest, extending learning or making an impact. Talk the same language as your backers.

Learning the language

A whole new set of terms have developed in recent years to describe the complete process of funding and managing projects. Here are twenty five of the main terms used:

Added Value. The term added value is used to show how initial investment is enhanced or added to by what the project does with it. For example, a government scheme may provide funds of £30,000 for a project managed by a local agency. The agency uses volunteers, local contacts and expertise to deliver the project. These factors 'add value' to the original £30,000. It is possible to suggest an equivalent cash value of the added value factors.

Additionality. Similar to added value, but usually referring to adding extra income. Initial funding to a project may be regarded as pump priming that aims to bring in other resources.

● CASE STUDY

The long decision

In one fairly typical local authority a national charity submitted a proposal to run a small project costing £18,000. There was strong support within the authority for the project - indeed a senior manager had put forward a bid. The timetable from early discussions to project agreement was over eighteen months. Here is the chain of events:

January. Meetings with senior manager, chair and vice chair of the relevant service committee to discuss the project. Councillors and assistant director visit and are impressed with a similar project. No chance of funding until next financial year. Decisions on available funding have already been made.

Late February. Urgent activity. Possibility that the department may have underspent this year. The chance that the project could be started on this underspend was explored but no progress.

April. New financial year.

May. Council Annual General Meeting appoints new committee chairs. Meeting with the departmental assistant director to see if the project could be included in a package of projects in a central government Single Regeneration Budget. The possibility of funding the project from the National Lottery is raised and dismissed.

June. The project will not go into the Single Regeneration Bid. Does not fit the current criteria. The departmental director briefs the new chair and vice chair about the departmental strategic plan. The project is identified as being a medium to high priority. Over the summer reports show that the council needs to make up to 5% savings in all service areas.

September. The charity is invited to contribute to a short training session for relevant departmental staff on the experience of the project. A meeting with the assistant director is positive. The project will go forward as one of the department's main bids.

October. The key councillors in the controlling party review future plans and back the plan provided officers find a way of reallocating current spending.

November. Charity asked to prepare and present business plan to council officers. Detailed discussion about costings, service plans and how the project fits with the department's priorities and existing services.

January. Positive indications that there may be space in the budget following a reorganisation.

February. Charity makes short presentation to council sub committee. Spending proposal discussed in the controlling political group and Policy and Resources Committee. Charity asked to produce a scaled down project as a contingency measure.

March. Council budget approved including a slightly reduced project budget. Negotiations with officers on the service contract between the charity and the council.

Three points are worth noting about this process:

❶ The charity spent most of its time building a relationship from which funding for a project would develop. It did not see the issue as simply being about fundraising.

❷ The internal process within the authority was complex. Power was shared between several different parties. The charity needed to find out about how decisions were made and how influence could best be exercised. It needed to find a key player, in this case an assistant director.

❸ The process took time. On occasion the charity thought that the project would not happen. They had to be prepared to make some changes to the design and time scales of the project to fit with the authority's interests. Managing this was particularly hard as they were concerned that they could lose the distinctiveness of the project.

Business Case. A business case is used to set out the economic, organisational and overall benefits involved in a new activity. The business case is usually written by the bidder and is really a scaled-down version of a feasibility study and a business plan.

Business Plan. A written plan setting out the background, goals, strategy, financial and resource details of the project for the immediate future. The business plan makes the case for the organisation by setting out its strategy, intended activities and management arrangements. A business plan can last anywhere between one to five years.

Criteria. The published statement of priorities and requirements that bidders need to follow to be successful in gaining backing.

Core funding. The general non-project costs involved in running an organisation. Typical core costs would include administration, management support and general overhead costs. It is usually harder to raise money for core costs.

Delivery Plan. A statement of targeted outputs and outcomes that a project should achieve.

End date. The agreed set date upon which the project or a key phase should cease.

Evaluation. Evaluation looks at either the project's process (how it works) or the project's programme (what it delivers) to see if it meets its original goals and objectives.

Exit strategy. A plan of what will happen at the end of the project and how the project will close down.

Impact. What difference the project is able to effect. Often impact is the link between the project's outputs and the project's longer term outcomes.

Inputs. The resources (finance, equipment and other resources) directed into a project.

Leverage. The process by which the project brings in other money. Several government schemes require bids to describe how, if successful, they will lever in private sector money.

Match funding. Several funders, including some of the National Lottery Distribution Boards require bidders to put together a package of funding. They would fund a project up to a certain amount provided other income is guaranteed from other sources.

Milestones. Key events marking a clear stage in completing a main stage of the project. Sometimes the term landmark is used instead.

Outputs. What the project produces and delivers. Outputs are usually physical or measurable items.

Outcomes. The benefits and overall difference that the project makes.

Performance measurement. Preset measures or indicators by which the outputs and outcomes of the project will be measured.

Project appraisal. The process of evaluating a proposed project to see if it is worth investing in.

Quality assurance. Evidence of clear minimum standards showing the minimum levels of service and practice that should always operate.

Sustainable benefits. Evidence that the longer term impact and effect of the project has been thought about. Once a sustainable project has ended, other things (services, activities and relationships) should still be able to carry on.

Synergy. How projects work together, avoid duplication of effort and create partnerships.

Targets. Preset outputs or outcomes that the project should aim to meet.

Value For Money. A study of a project to check that the inputs are planned on a sound economic base, that the outputs are efficiently managed and that the outcomes are worthwhile and effective in meeting the original purpose or need.

Vision statement. A broad statement of the overall goals and values that underpin the project.

Build the relationship

Be clear what kind of relationship potential backers want and need.
Four types of relationships are possible:

◆ Benevolent supporter
◆ Collaborator
◆ Investor
◆ Client/Purchaser

All of these relationships need different kinds of relationship building and approaches. There may also be some considerable overlap.

Different types of funders, purchasers and backers

Benevolent supporter

Relationship: Prepared to stand back from the project, trust it to organise its affairs and be happy to be periodically kept in touch with news and developments

Key words: Funder, Donation, Commitment

How to involve: Keep in touch with the project through personal visits, contacts and news. Show that the project is a worthy and sound idea to fund

Collaborator

Relationship: An active desire to work with the project and possibly participate in its management and organisation. Needs to be included in key decisions and negotiate a visible profile within the project

Key words: Partner, Multi agency working, Key stake holder

How to involve: Can be involved through membership of steering groups, planning meetings and as someone with whom the project regularly consults. Be careful of too much involvement in detailed management issues

Investor

Relationship: A background role, but with a clear interest in the longer term outcomes and differences that the project creates. Do not wish to be involved in the detail, but will take a keen interest in the project's results

Key words: Outcomes, Added value, Measurable impact

How to involve: Needs to be involved from the start in agreeing the success criteria and in discussing outcomes. Need to keep them in touch with progress and results. Good evaluation and evidence is important

Client/Purchaser

Relationship: Sees the project as supplying a service or activity which it needs in accordance with a clear agreement. They need to see exact monitoring and measurement and will be concerned about the project's direct performance

Key words: The contract specification, Value for money, Monitoring

How to involve: The negotiation of the contract will create a formal relationship. Work will also be needed to create good communication and understanding. The project may have to help contract officers appreciate what the project actually does

Maintain the relationship

Many commercial businesses make the mistake of pursuing new business rather than consolidating and maintaining their existing customer base. Obtaining new business is expensive and time consuming compared to keeping what you already have. A key part of a funding strategy is to establish how to maintain and consolidate existing relationships by involving, communicating and working with existing backers. They should be seen as long term investors not completed sales.

Getting the project going

Creating momentum for a project

A new project needs to be able to move fast. It also needs to be able to involve other people, create alliances and support and make people feel that they have an investment in the project's success. The group (and at this stage it needs to be a group rather than one individual) at the centre of the project needs to be able to juggle many different activities. They need to be able to make decisions on legal structures, organisational matters and financial issues and at the same time create a feeling of energy and excitement around the project.

In this stage the people steering a new project need to be able to drive the project and make sure that it makes progress. They also need to create an effective style and process for the way that the project works. The perceived success of a project is sometimes badly affected by how it relates to and involves people and agencies not directly involved in the project. All too often the people steering a new project work on it in isolation. They do not test or communicate their ideas. No one knows what they are doing. They spring surprises on people. Sometimes the people developing new projects within an organisation are seen as being out of touch, and even arrogant. The project idea may well be imaginative and sound, but the way in which people learn of it, are introduced to it and involved in it is crucial to the project's success.

In this phase three factors need to happen:

- The project must take on an organised form
- The commitment and enthusiasm of the people around the project must be maintained
- The project must reach out to and involve other people.

The project must make progress, it has deadlines to reach and work to be done. The people steering the project need to become an effective team; they must be able to work together and make decisions quickly. However, for the project to work it must inform and involve other people.

The balance can easily be lost. Too much consultation and participation can delay decisions and stall progress. If the core team becomes too inward looking and adopts too strong an 'internal culture' then it can put off others who need to be involved. Equally, the more people who are involved in a project, the harder it is to make decisions quickly and maintain a sense of ownership.

Projects at this stage need to build up momentum. They need to have organised the different tasks that need completing to get the project up and running. Responsibilities for making and carrying out decisions must be clearly understood. Progress needs to be monitored and early warning systems developed to ensure that if something is taking too long, action can be taken to remedy it. Three things can be useful to help a project become task oriented:

Explicit rules about delegation, responsibility and accountability. In people-based organisations decision making is sometimes painful. A form of organisational ping pong is played. An issue is bounced around from meeting to meeting, working group to individual until it either runs out of steam or time. The issue becomes redundant. One health authority withdrew from contract negotiations to set up a community project with a voluntary organisation because it found it impossible to work with the representatives of the project. Every decision and development had to be referred to a management committee meeting that only met every few weeks. This dissipated the momentum behind the project.

Individuals should know exactly what they are responsible for, what decisions they can make and what they need to refer to others. Trust, good communication and accountability comes from clear rules rather than a vague commitment that 'we will all get on well together'.

A clear plan of what needs to be done. The activities involved in a project start-up can be vast. A useful process is to list them all and allocate priorities to them. Getting things in the right order is important. A visible and active planning system can help this, provided it is updated regularly and monitored.

Methods for marking progress and achievements. Progress seems to create more progress. In this phase it is important to build up a feeling that you are making progress and are on course. The steering group for an arts project started all of its meetings by working through a progress checklist and highlighting action and events. It looked at what was stopping progress and agreed the next steps. The inevitable problems that occur in a project's start-up may cast a shadow over the progress that is being made. This can demotivate and demoralise those involved.

A lot of the literature and research on teams overlooks the point that team work is hard work. It sounds nice, but often is not. People confuse team work with getting on with people. Teams degenerate into social meetings where several people meet and one or two people do all the work. However for all its problems, teamwork is important in developing a project. It stops the project being too closely identified with one person, it brings in different skills to the project and can strengthen it.

A former director of a large agency described how his organisation often ran into problems.

"We stressed teamwork. As early as possible staff working on a project were encouraged to work together and see it as their project. During the development stages they were often almost invisible from the rest of the organisation as they worked away getting the project on line. The problem came when the project was introduced to others in the organisation. It was usually sprung on them. People often complained that they did not know anything about the project until it had started operating. They did not know how it affected their work. Recently we have improved how we set up projects. One particularly successful project was a campaign which during the development stage managed to create a strong campaign team and at the same time a visible network of people in the organisation whose commitment to it and goodwill would be critical to its eventual success."

Effective team working does not just happen. The development of good team work needs to be encouraged. The following six points can help.

Good teams need a few clear rules

There is a paradox that the more flexibly and informally you choose to work the more important it is to have firm rules that everyone keeps to. Without some rules things fall apart and become anarchic. Commonly agreed rules are needed about decision making power, communication, accountability and responsibilities.

Teams welcome and use diversity

Team work is not about all being the same. People frequently join or are recruited to a project because they like, identify or fit with the other people. This is inevitable, but done to excess it can create an inward looking, 'clique' feel to the project. Good teams hold a common commitment to the project's vision and values, but are made up of people with different skills, backgrounds and experience. Good team work is not about everyone thinking and operating the same all of the time.

Teams need to know and exploit each member's skills

A useful team development tool is to ask each team member to complete a questionnaire auditing their skills, experience and contacts. This can be an enormous help to a new project. It can bring to light resources that were unknown and identify particular gaps that the project will need to fill.

Teams need to be focused on making progress

During the start-up phase of the project, the core group of people needs to be very task and goal oriented. They need to get the project up and running with firm and realistic targets.

The size of the team is important

Studies of effective teamwork suggest that after around ten to fifteen people a group finds it hard to operate as a team. It is difficult to communicate quickly, there is a lack of collective responsibility and accountability. It is harder to win agreement about how to work.

Teams use feedback, acknowledge progress and celebrate

Teams creating new projects need to keep themselves and the outside world informed of progress and achievements. One steering group of a new hostel produced a monthly 'project road map' as a way of identifying progress and problems and keeping their contacts informed. Progress should be acknowledged and celebrated as this creates the enthusiasm.

The invisible project team

Projects need to be able to do two things at once. They need to be able to build a core group which operates as a team and shows a sense of priority and commitment to the project. They also need to reach outwards and at an early stage build a strong network of contacts, friends, decision makers and opinion formers whose support and goodwill will be crucial to the project's success. This requires the project to market itself, inform people about what it is doing, enthuse them and encourage them to feel part of it. Many of the key people to contact here may have been identified in a feasibility study or when the decision to go ahead with the project was made. They include:

- Direct users. People who the project should benefit or involve at some stage.
- Supporters. People who will support it through investing time, money or lending their support.
- Decision makers. People who have an influence over its success.
- People indirectly affected by it. People whose relationship to the project will not be primary, but will still have an impact e.g. neighbours, other agencies etc.

In their book, **Project Leadership**, Briner, Geddes and Hastings refer to these people as an Invisible project team. They suggest that to neglect this invisible team is dangerous and will impede the chance of the project being successful.

Early identification and contact with this network can provide the following benefits:

There is often a direct relationship to the level of involvement that someone has had in the consultation and start-up phases and their attitude to the project's work. Early communication and involvement can help to overcome misgivings about the project and build support for it.

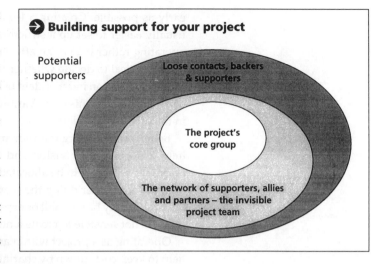

Building support for your project

Potential supporters

Loose contacts, backers & supporters

The project's core group

The network of supporters, allies and partners – the invisible project team

Some of the network can use their influence to help the project. They can open doors for the project. They can use their contacts, lend credibility and support. The network stops the project from 'operating in the dark'. People around the project can be used to test out plans and can provide the project with valuable insights. They can stop the project springing unwanted products on people.

The process of building and sustaining this network can be carried out by:

- Using individuals as sounding boards for ideas as the project develops
- Running focus groups to consult with key people
- Producing newsletters and bulletins to keep people informed about the project
- Organising presentations, seminars and open days to build the relationship
- Carrying out surveys to gauge opinion about the project's priorities, plans and goals
- Asking people in the network for help and expertise
- Asking people in the network to pilot or try out the project's product on a trial basis

Creating an appropriate legal structure for the project

As the project moves from being an idea to an organised form, important decisions need to be taken about what sort of legal structure is needed. It is best that this sort of decision is made as early as possible. Creating a legal structure takes time and it is usually easier to set up a structure before the project has started operating rather than as an afterthought.

It is critical to decide whether the project should be a separate legal organisation independent of any others or a constituent part of an existing organisation. Various factors need to be considered in making this decision.

Being a separate organisation may create a strong identity and help to form a clear vision and direction. However, time and resources will have to be allocated to setting up and running the organisation rather doing the work of the project. In some cases the project may be so small or expected to have so short a lifespan that it is not sensible to create a new organisation.

Operating as a project within an established organisation may help to keep costs down by sharing overheads and may make the project feel stronger. If the established organisation is an effective one then the project should be able to benefit from its contacts, expertise and management support. On the other hand the project's identity and focus may be lost within a larger agency. The project's reputation and direction could be constrained or even damaged by the parent body.

A possible half-way house solution is to place the project in an established organisation during its first few years with a clear agreement that after a certain time it will emerge as an independent body. Several organisations have started like this and several national and local development agencies such as Councils for Voluntary Services have developed some skills and experience in housing new projects.

The implications of being a project within an organisation

One of the most lively debates in organisational development in recent years has been the relationship within organisations between the centre and local units. Traditionally, organisations have been designed around command and control. The centre made most decisions, allocated and controlled resources and expected local units and projects to follow their line. In recent years, things have changed most notably in the private sector and some parts of the public sector. Much more delegation, independence and autonomy to act has been given to local projects.

In deciding to create a project within an organisation issues of power, responsibility and delegation need to be agreed. Failure to do so can create major problems. A group of teachers and educational psychologists developed a new way of working with difficult children. They were encouraged by a national charity to let the charity develop and manage their idea. A project was set up with staff employed by the charity and line managed by one of the charity's regional offices. The original group was involved in recruiting the staff and was invited to form an advisory group to support the project. One of the original group members described the problems that started to emerge a few months after the project started operating:

"The project workers ended up being pulled between us and the regional office. There were a whole series of misunderstandings about good practice, values and direction. The managers from the regional office looked at things differently from us and at the end of the day they have the line management and financial power to direct the project. The advisory group is toothless".

For a project to fit well within an organisation the following factors need attention:

Compatibility between the organisation's aims, objectives and values and the project's vision and values

The project must fit with the organisational, constitutional and managerial objectives. The project needs to have similar values and goals to the rest of the organisation. There needs to be a synergy of purpose. There also needs to be a compatibility between the style, values and aspirations of the project and the sponsoring organisation.

Compatibility between the different projects that the organisation runs

The project should complement other projects that the organisation sponsors. A large service delivery agency agreed to take on a project promoting user advocacy and rights. Some of the work of the new project was perceived by other staff as being against them. It encouraged their users to make complaints and demand more rights. It created conflict between projects. The new project did not fit with the rest of the agency.

Clear agreement about delegation and policy

Often in organisations it is assumed that rules and policies are clearly understood. You only find out that they exist when you step over them. Projects need to know the boundaries which apply to them. They need to be clear about what is delegated to them, what decisions they can make and what issues need to be approved by the parent organisation.

Clear agreement about the management and use of resources

Increasingly organisations are making their budgets cost or activity centred, to show the full cost of operating a project. Done properly this can show the real cost of the project, the cost to the sponsor organisation of managing it and encourage the project manager to exercise proper control.

Clear arrangements for employing and managing staff

Staff working in projects need to understand to whom and for what they are accountable. One national agency ran into several problems on this point. It encouraged local involvement in its community work projects and as part of that insisted that projects had local 'management committees' made up of local users and partners. The terms of reference for the committees were never clear. Staff were employed by the national body and line managed by its staff. However in two instances, active local committee members operated as if staff were accountable to them. Confusion and conflict regularly ensued.

One useful idea is to set out the management relationship between a project and the sponsoring organisation. This can be particularly helpful if you want the project to operate at arms length from the main organisation or if there is a strong possibility that at some stage in the future the project could become fully independent. In the public sector this type of document (usually called a service level agreement) is common between service and support departments. It sets out measurable expectations in terms of service and standards. Possible headings for such a document include:

- **Scope of the arrangement.** That the document is intended to clarify the internal management arrangement. It is not a legal contract.
- **The relationship between the organisation and the project.** That the project is a constituent part of the organisation and as such is controlled by its policies and rules.
- **Management responsibilities**. A description of what kinds of support, resources and supervision the sponsoring organisation is responsible for providing.
- **Staff management arrangements**. That the line management and employment responsibility is with the sponsoring organisation.
- **Management charge.** How much the sponsoring organisation intends to charge the project internally in respect of its management costs and as a contribution to shared and organisational overheads.

◆ **Resource management issues**. How budgets are delegated to and controlled by the project.

◆ **Involvement of any third parties**. How other parties such as user groups and funders should relate to the project and the main organisation.

◆ **Review arrangements**. How and when the project and the arrangement be reviewed.

It is unlikely that this document would be regarded as a legal arrangement as it is not drawn up between two separate legal entities; rather it is a framework for management and supervision.

Becoming a separate legal entity

Creating a project with a separate legal identity independent of any other organisation involves five main stages. Before these stages can be started, one or two individuals must be appointed and have the time and access to external help to steer it through.

◆ Decide whether the organisation is to be an incorporated body (usually a company limited by guarantee) or if it will be an unincorporated body

◆ Clarify whether the organisation's purposes are charitable

◆ Get advice and draft an appropriate governing document (constitution)

◆ Decide who will be on the first governing body (management committee)

◆ If appropriate, register as a company and/or charity

This can be a time-consuming and complex business. It involves understanding different aspects of law and making sure that individuals are fully aware of their individual and collective duties. It is useful to take advice at an early stage and discuss with an experienced adviser the different options, responsibilities and implications. Several national networks have produced model constitutions which should speed the process. For example the charity Community Matters produces a model constitution for community associations. The Charity Commission also provides model documents for charitable companies, trusts and associations. Local Councils for Voluntary Service or Rural Community Councils should be able to help.

Legal structures for projects with charitable objectives

The main legal distinction between structures is between being an incorporated organisation or an unincorporated organisation. An incorporated organisation has a legal identity independent of its members or trustees. It can enter into contracts and own property in its own right. An unincorporated body is recognised

---

Legal structures for independent projects

Two separate issues:

Issue 1
Should the project be an incorporated body or should it remain an unincorporated body?

Issue 2
Are the objectives of the project wholly charitable?

in law only as a group of individuals. As a body it has no separate legal status so, for example, property is held in the name of the trustees as individuals on behalf of the organisation. Any contracts are entered into by individuals acting on behalf of all members.

The main forms of unincorporated bodies are:

◆ **An unincorporated association** such as a club, society or similar association.
◆ **A trust** formed to pursue a purpose whereby individuals agree to act on trust to ensure that resources are used for the purposes prescribed. A trust is generally not a membership organisation.

The main forms of incorporated bodies used by charities are:

◆ **A company limited by guarantee**, where its members guarantee to provide a set amount (usually £1) if the company becomes insolvent.
◆ **An Industrial and Provident Society** (IPS) set up to trade as a bona fide cooperative or for the benefits of the community.

Charitable status

Registration as a charity is a separate issue from the question of unincorporation and corporation. If an organisation's objectives are all wholly charitable as defined in law and it expects to have an annual income of £10,000 it must register with the Charity Commission in England and Wales or apply to the Inland Revenue for recognition in Scotland or Northern Ireland.

Charities enjoy significant tax advantages and credibility in fund raising. Having charitable objectives does place legal requirements on charitable trustees to ensure that the charity operates within charity law and also puts limits on particular types of political activities.

It is common for many voluntary organisations to register as both a charity and also to become a company limited by guarantee. Such a charity must then act within both charity and company law.

The Governing Body

All organisations have a governing body. Often they are called management committees or boards. If the organisation is a charity the voting members of this body are charitable trustees. If the organisation is registered as a company the directors are charitable trustees. Members of the body have a responsibility to understand the law as it relates to their organisation and to have a broad awareness of any contractual obligations or any other legal obligations such as leases and employment contracts. Failure to comply with the law could lead to civil and in some cases criminal action against individual members of the governing body. Failure to understand and monitor contracts could place the organisation in financial or other legal difficulties. If the organisation is unincorporated and cannot meet its debts, members could be made personally liable.

In deciding upon and dealing with issues of legal structures the following four points need attention:

Drafting the constitution is important

For an independent project the constitution is a critical document. It provides a framework for decision making, governance and management. Drafting it should not be seen as a legalistic chore. A useful way of studying a draft is to ask 'what if...' questions such as 'what if we wanted to merge with another organisation?' or 'how and when should the committee be elected?' The constitution should guide you through most everyday problems and situations.

The right to know

Many committee members only find out about responsibilities placed on them by accident. In some situations they find out far too late. At the start of the project proper training and background information in governing the organisation and in legal and financial liabilities should be given. This should be repeated for new members of the committee.

Liabilities can be personal

Failure to meet legal obligations under both charity and company law can in severe cases carry criminal penalties and/or personal liabilities for debts. Responsibilities, obligations and their implications need to be discussed openly and honestly from the outset and the various types of insurance must be fully considered.

Sound management is vital

No legal structure can replace the need for accountability, effective communication and clear expectations between the governing body and the project's staff, users, volunteers and funders. Relying on trust and goodwill is not enough. It is easier and much more sensible to agree clear boundaries for making decisions, reporting lines and information flows at the start of a project rather than in response to a crisis. Members of the governing body have the ultimate responsibility for the project.

All decisions with significant or long term financial and legal implications must be made by the governing body. They cannot be abdicated or delegated to staff.

Developing a strategy for the project

During this stage an outline strategy for the project needs to take shape. Strategy is an overused word, used without clear definition or explanation. Many published strategies are far too vague and unrealistic. They avoid making difficult decisions about priorities and resources. Good strategy has three elements:

◆ It links the project's overall vision and what it does in practice
◆ It is about making priorities. Strategy should answer the question – how can we best use our resources to make the best impact?
◆ It sets out a clear direction for the project to follow

The detail of the strategy will be developed in the project's budget, business plan and work programme. At this stage it is important to agree a direction and statement of priorities for the project's first year or first few years. In developing this strategy it is important to think realistically. The strategy needs to be informed by the following:

How can we make the best impact with the resources available?

Mission and vision statements are not meant to give any sense of immediate direction. They are meant to provide an overall statement of purpose. Strategy should be concerned with impact and effectiveness. It should also link what you want to do and what you can do.

What can we do and what are other people best able to do?

Good strategy is informed by the outside world. In drawing up an outline strategy think carefully about how your project should fit with other agencies. How do you avoid duplication of effort? How can you create useful working relationships with others?

How do we keep the project distinctive?

With a new project it is usually important that it has a strong identity. It will need to market and sell itself effectively. How will the project consolidate its unique selling proposition of the project?

What should be our priorities?

The most difficult part of any discussion around strategy is agreeing what you are not going to do rather that agreeing what you are going to do. Once you have agreed your strategy there will probably be several activities and ideas that will have been dropped, discarded or postponed. Trying to do too many things kills many new projects. A few realistic priorities to work on are much more useful than a vague wish list.

What should be the balance of our work?

A new project should be able to identify several different types of work. Some activities within the project will be experimental and innovative. Others will be long term and permanent. Some activities will be about service provision, others could be more about campaigning for change. A good strategy should create a manageable portfolio of different types of work.

Formulating a project's strategy

Be consistent about terminology

There is no clear definition about the hierarchy or exact meaning of terms such as aims, goals and objectives. Sometimes the term objectives is used to describe the overarching purpose of a project. Others believe that objectives refer to the detailed and specific actions needed at any one time. Make sure that your use of such terms is defined and followed.

The plan should cascade down and should follow a logical order. It is helpful to think of a plan as having three levels:

- Overall vision and purpose - the mission statement
- Strategic direction - main priorities and aims
- Detailed objectives - the work plan for the project.

The mission statement sets out the overall vision and purpose of the project. It should briefly describe what the project is for and what it aims to do. The statement of strategic direction should give the project a clear guide as to what are its main priorities at any one time. From this it should be possible to draw up work plans, action lists and commit resources to a fixed timetable.

The mission statement should last throughout the project. Some parts of the strategy may last throughout the project, but priorities and direction will change periodically. The mission statement should not need constant reappraisal. The project's strategy should be reviewed at least annually. It should be sharp and set out an agreed direction. The objectives should be developed from the strategy. The objectives should be task oriented, measurable and indicate who is responsible for delivering them.

Build in flexibility

Often project strategies are far too detailed. Possibly to impress or reassure funders every pound is allocated and every hour is planned. Certainly in the first year of the project it will be hard to programme everything. Retain some flexibility. The project needs a firm direction for its start-up and for its first year. Effective project leadership is about operating flexibly within the overall plan.

Keep it measurable

Good measurement is important. It creates the feeling of making progress, it pinpoints problems and blocks and it provides useful feedback and management information. The statement of direction and the detailed tactical issues all need to be written in such a way that you are aware of what progress is being made and can identify achievements.

Assign responsibilities throughout

The strategy should indicate what is going to happen and who is responsible for it. It is easier to agree responsibilities before something goes wrong or does not happen rather than afterwards.

Focus on results

The language of the strategy must be practical, task oriented and precise. It should be about what will happen and what will be delivered rather than the detailed activities needed to get there. It should focus on the project's outputs and outcomes.

➔ A project strategy checklist

☐ **Does it follow on from an agreed vision?**
The strategy should be influenced by the original vision that led to the project being set up. It should be guided by the vision rather than by what funding might be available or what you or your colleagues feel most confident about doing!

☐ **Is it based on an analysis of the world outside?**
The strategy should be based on an informed understanding of what is happening in the project's environment. All too often strategies are drawn up with scant regard for the world outside. Planning needs to follow from and be informed by an honest analysis and appraisal of the project's environment.

☐ **Does it set out a definite direction for the project?**
The strategy should enable you to do detailed planning. It should indicate both priorities and things that might well be important, but cannot be current priorities. Good strategies will indicate what you are not going to do as much as what you are going to do. They are realistic.

☐ **Does it inform how you budget for and structure the project?**
Questions of structure and resources should follow the agreement of a project's strategy, not dictate it. How you organise and how you intend to spend money should be determined by the strategy.

☐ **Is it clearly understood?**
Can most people connected to the project summarise the key elements of the strategy? Will individuals use the project's strategy to guide and inform the details of their work? Can you summarise it in three or four headlines?

☐ **Is it measurable?**
Is the strategy written down in a clear enough way that you will be able to measure the performance and progress of the project against it? Does it indicate key milestones? Does it help you to establish a success criteria for the project?

Agreeing critical success factors for the project

A useful technique to focus a project is to identify what are its critical success factors. Critical success factors are the key issues that need to be in place for the project to work. The process of agreeing critical success factors clarifies thinking, opens up communication amongst the project team and should help to coordinate and bring together effort and activity. It is best to only have a handful of critical success factors. Too many and they will lose their significance.

Examples of critical success factors are:

External relations

"We need a high media profile"

"We must build strong links with other bodies in our field"

"We have to develop a positive relationship with our main backers"

Internal

"A key factor is to sustain and develop a strong volunteer team"

"We need to build the management skills of all unit leaders"

"We must introduce a faster and reliable management information system"

Style

"We have to encourage a culture that is innovative and allows risk"

"We must keep the vision and values relevant and clear as the project expands"

"We must find ways of listening to and learning from our users"

Information and communication

"We have to find reliable formal communication between our three bases"

" We have to be able to explain the project to new people in a succinct way"

" We must improve the quality of our communication to the outside world"

The critical success factors will change as the project develops. They set a leadership and management agenda for the project. Getting a project going involves a myriad of complex and demanding tasks and processes. It is easy to be sucked into being incredibly busy or to become obsessed with controlling and managing everything. The art of management is in knowing what are the main factors that need attention at any one time.

Using milestones to identify progress

In this stage it is worth identifying some key milestones to use to measure progress. The steering group of a local children's charity identified five key milestones to achieve its goal of setting up a family centre:

1. Appointed trustees, applied for charity registration and started fundraising
2. Appointed management group, consultants and freelance fund raiser
3. Achieved income commitments up to £55,000
4. Leased building and started to advertise for staff
5. Agreed open date and planned launch

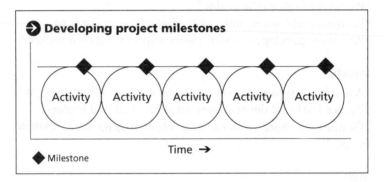

→ Developing project milestones

Activity Activity Activity Activity Activity

◆ Milestone

Time →

The time between each milestone varied considerably. This is how the chair of the trustees assessed their value: *'The milestones gave a discipline to our work. They provided a focus to our activity and stopped us galloping ahead. At each milestone the trustees reviewed progress and made sure that we were in a fit state to move onto the next set of tasks'.*

Milestones work best if they are linked to the completion of key tasks. They are a landmark for the start-up phase. It is useful to agree an anticipated date when you expect a milestone to be achieved.

On reaching a milestone the following things should happen:

- **Progress is reviewed.** Achieving the milestone shows that you are making progress. It is useful to spend time assessing the work done so far to establish what works and what does not and to identify any learning points.
- **The project original brief is validated.** In reaching the milestone you may have learned something that changes the original assumptions and thinking behind the project outline. Are the original plans still sound? Is the success criteria still attainable?

What changes in how you envisage the project working might be necessary?

♦ **The detail for the next stage is agreed**. The milestone review should be a useful opportunity to agree the who, what, when and how of the next stage of the project's start-up. Plans should be drawn up which will take the project to the next milestone.

♦ **Progress is monitored and celebrated**. Acknowledging progress is something at which many of us are bad. Milestones are commonplace in some industries. In the building trade when brick work reaches roof height a milestone called 'topping out' is reached. A celebration is sometimes had. This acknowledges work so far completed and gives people a feeling of making headway.

Designing the project

Often projects are not designed. They are thrown together to meet fast approaching deadlines. This chapter puts forward some practical ideas about how projects can be designed and outlines some new ways of organising work. Four features make the design of projects important and different from how organisations have traditionally been established and managed:

◆ Projects need to be designed for organisational flexibility rather than permanence
◆ Projects need structures and systems which enable them to move quickly rather than simply control resources
◆ Projects need to be aware of the full costs of their activities
◆ Many projects are of a fixed term duration. There is a clear point in the future when the project will end

New thinking about work and how we organise

Most of today's organisations were designed to be permanent rather than carry out short-term or project-based work. They were intended to minimise change and allow for command and control from the top down. They worked fairly well provided little changed. They provided continuity, certainty and control.

Key principles of the 'old-style' organisational design were:

A clear hierarchical structure

Policy and strategy making was carried out at the top. Service delivery was at the bottom. Some thought and others acted. Often the number of levels or compartments in a structure grew rapidly. Very tight spans of control were created. The more contact you had with the user the less rewards you received. Resources such as finance were held centrally and tightly controlled.

Tight boundaries

Most organisations used departmental, professional or geographic divides as the key organisational building blocks. You knew your job and you kept to it. This often created tension within the organisation as different groups clashed and played out office politics or work fell between two places.

➡ Old and new organisational design ideas

Old ideas	New ideas
Built to last	Built to change
Designed to be permanent	Designed to be flexible
Need to cope with incremental change	Need to live with constant change Don't assume that anything will stay the same
Strict hierarchy of control	Networks
Command and control from the top down	Everything should be task oriented
Job descriptions highly defined	Flexible job roles
Status and position important	Emphasis on teams
Detailed plans and budgets	Strategic thinking
Strong belief in long term paper planning	Must be able to spot external trends and quickly respond to them
Tight control of all resources	Resources must be managed flexibly to meet changes
Central control	Much more delegation and devolution of power and resources
Uniform employment systems	Variety of employment arrangements
Standard employment rules and conditions for all	Increased use of short term contracts, freelance staff, associates and secondments as and when needed

Communication came from the top down

Little formal communication went back up and across the organisation.

Constant changes have found these design principles to be lacking. New needs emerge faster. Technology is changing how we can work. Changes in policy, funding and the external environment seem to happen much more frequently.

"So much of what we call management consists of making it difficult for people to work."

Peter F Drucker

Narrow job design, strict boundaries and top heavy structures made change, team work and flexibility difficult. Traditional thinking about management also produced a fragmented organisation in which few people saw the whole picture. Instead people only saw their bit of it.

Organisations today

Projects need to be designed with the following four features in mind:

- **The project needs to be focused on results.** People and resources must be used flexibly within the project to meet its end. The project needs to be geared up to meet its tasks rather than simply exist within the structure.
- **Everyone in the project must see the big picture.** Projects usually have very flat structures so everyone can keep in touch and feel part of the project. Everyone involved in the project must feel committed to the whole of the project and not just their part of it.
- **The project's structure must enable it to change as required.** Projects go through different phases. The kind of work needed in the start-up phase will be different from work needed in the main part of the project or at its end. Staff roles and responsibilities need to be adaptable. Many aspects of the project will be temporary rather than fixed.
- **Team work as a building block.** In smaller projects staff need to be flexible in how they operate and will often work without much direct supervision. Projects need to consider recruiting people who are experienced in being part of a team, are able to cover for and support other team members and possibly can become multi-skilled.

Strategy versus structure

There are not many established rules on how to design an organisation. One of the few well-established ones is that decisions first need to be made about strategy (i.e. what you are going to do) before you agree the structure and systems of how you are going to do it.

Often the structures and systems we have restrict and limit the strategy that we can follow. Badly-designed job descriptions, staff structures and other systems can get in the way of the project.

A director of a specialist advice agency described their experience of this issue:

"When we set up the project we made very quick decisions about what sort of jobs we would need. We recruited people for their particular

technical competence. We started out with three individuals who were experts in their own fields. However, the project's plan requires them to take on pieces of work that require a broad range of skills. Often they have to work as trainers or local advisers and operate outside of their specialist boundary. The job roles that we agreed and recruited against have created a structure that works against our strategy".

Structural and system factors such as job roles, reporting relationships, budget and resource controls and even factors such as office layouts all have a major impact on how we work. They need, therefore, to be designed after you have agreed the overall strategic direction and priorities for the project.

Structures and systems need to fit the project, rather than the project having to fit in with the structures and systems that exist. This can be done by:

Developing the project's structure

Often when we design a new project we are inclined to copy how large and established organisations work. One new campaign group was set up by a group of activists who mainly worked in large public sector organisations. They drafted out a project structure which had a committee structure that reflected their experience of working in a large organisation. The staff team spent most of its first year struggling to service the organisational bureaucracy and controls. The new campaign director had to fight hard to persuade them to reduce the number of meetings and standing sub committees from six to two, renegotiate staff job descriptions to include flexibility as a main task and reduce the amount of paper reports required.

The following eight points are useful in building a flexible project structure:

Make delegation of responsibilities and decision making explicit

Often lines of responsibility are never made clear. The boundary of what you can do, how much money you can spend or what decisions you can make only become clear once you get it wrong. It is easier to agree and review boundaries in advance rather than after a problem. Good delegation should include tasks (i.e. what work you have to do) and what decisions you can make. Some organisations are very good at delegating (or even dumping) work, but not so good at delegating decision making power.

Keep the remit of committees focused

The remit and responsibilities of management boards or committees need to be agreed and documented. People need to be clear what decisions need to be made by the committee and what information the committee need to make informed decisions.

Watch out for a 'democratic overload'

Even in quite small projects meetings can take over. Sub-committees and working groups are formed to work on an issue or even as a way of pretending to make progress. With the exception of the main management committee, the need for committees, sub groups and meetings should be looked at regularly. If they are not 'adding value' to the project and simply have become part of an organisational routine they should be stood down.

Budget for flexibility

Projects often need a budgeting system that allows for some flexibility. The project may need to move cash between budget headings to allow for changed pattern of needs. The project may need occasional access to funds to develop new work and follow up opportunities. Certainly in the first year or so the budget should be able to support reasonable flexibility.

Identify relevant performance measures

To monitor the project's work and ensure progress towards its milestones and overall goals measurement is important. The management committee should agree some simple measures to ensure that it is informed of progress. Be careful of having too many measures. A few well chosen measures should act as a project's dashboard to help it to steer and alert it to any problems.

Use information technology intelligently

Most organisations have computers. However in offices, most computers are grossly under used. Often the use of technology is not planned. Training and support is not budgeted for. Technology is only used to automate what was previously done by hand. The potential of electronic mail to aid communication, and databases and other systems to help with other tasks is often overlooked. Seeing technology as a vital part of the project's organisation and planning how best to use it from the outset can be time saving.

Control paperwork

Several organisations are drowning in paper work. From the start encourage people to communicate in plain English. Avoid long reports and unnecessary systems and procedures.

Build in periodic organisational reviews

It is useful early on in a project to review how well the organisational systems and structures are helping to achieve the project's strategy. Three times a year one health agency holds a two hour organisational 'fitness workshop'. Blocks and barriers to effective teamwork, communication and progress are identified and eliminated. Even in a small agency unnecessary systems and bureaucracy can creep up quickly.

Common project design faults

Often organisations create structures that do not work. Here are some common ones:

The one-person organisation

When is a project too small to be an effective organisation? The sole employee of a self help agency described her role as "project director, fund raiser, ideas person, administrator, editor, office cleaner, bookkeeper and anything else that is thrown at me". The project worker had so many roles and expectations placed on her that the job was impossible. Everything depended on her. The management committee were committed but lacked the time to give support. Most of the employee's time was spent on keeping the organisation together rather than providing direct services. Often she was isolated, did not feel part of anything and lacked access to any support or supervision.

Rather than becoming a separate project the committee might have explored ways of housing the project within an existing organisation or contracting out some of the activities. Projects built around one key worker only work if there is considerable support and supervision with review mechanisms built in.

The top-heavy project

As part of a time management course the three workers of an education project recorded how they actually spent their time in quarter hourly intervals. They were shocked to learn that nearly 60% of their combined time went on servicing the organisation, attending meetings and preparing reports. The project had allowed a system of meetings, committees, reports and other aspects of internal bureaucracy to grow and multiply. It had an organisational structure that was far too big and time consuming in proportion to the size and work of the project.

Systems and structures are important, but do have a habit of propagating. Meetings take place because they are scheduled rather than needed, long reports look better than shorter ones and technology provides information that is rarely used, but looks interesting. It is worthwhile to regularly check the balance between time spent on direct or primary activities and time spent on indirect or internal activities. It is also useful to periodically prune administrative systems and processes.

The open-ended job

Job descriptions are usually written to make sure that every possible activity is included to prevent conflicts. Too often, new post holders have to spend the first few months of the project working out exactly what the job is for. Vague titles (such as 'development officer') and long lists of possible tasks give little clue as to what is really important in the job and what kind of impact you need to make. All too often individuals do the part of the job that they like or understand best.

It is important to be clear exactly what is expected of a job. What difference can an individual make? What should be their priorities? How will you measure success? Well written descriptions, efficient inductions and probationary reviews for new workers, regular reviews and work planning can all help to overcome this problem.

The powerless assistant/deputy

Often as a project expands it fails to think about its structure but simply adds to it. A common way of doing this is to give the hard pressed, senior person in the project a deputy or assistant as a way of helping them. A deputy or assistant type role can only work if certain tasks are clearly delegated to the deputy and there is some autonomy for the deputy. All too often deputies and assistants become human 'dumping grounds' for things that their boss no longer wants to do. They lack any independent authority or power. They are an understudy.

Rather than creating a deputy or assistant role it is better to review how tasks and responsibilities can be reallocated amongst existing staff and if needed to create a new post with clear responsibilities and tasks. They may still report to the senior person, but not as a stand in.

Issue = job

One national agency has a track record that whenever it identifies a policy or controversial issue it creates a job (or if it is a big issue a whole project) around the issue. Over the past ten years it has created an equal opportunities project, user involvement officer and most recently an environmental issues project. Setting up these projects creates an illusion that the agency is committed to and making progress on the issue. The reality is different. In all cases new post holders have to spend time trying to define exactly what is expected of them. In several cases by the time they have been appointed the organisation has lost interest in the issue and moved onto other things.

Good projects and good jobs are task rather than 'policy issue' oriented. If you cannot measure performance, identify criteria for success or define the desired outcomes clearly, then further thinking and discussion is urgently needed. Probably the worst thing to do would be to move straight to action and create a project.

Sealed containers in the organisation

A local housing agency grew in the traditional pattern. It created jobs and then departments based around the traditional job areas - housing management, maintenance, finance, development and director's office. Very quickly the five departments started to define how they wanted to organise their work. Over time it became obvious that tenants had to deal with several individuals to get a problem solved. In the old days one person could assess it, plan it and if not do it themselves call in a contractor. In the new situation, issues were referred to different departments. They all had their own systems and procedures. Delays, paperwork and conflicts between departments have increased.

As a project grows it is important to check that the structure and system supports the task rather than becomes an activity in itself. A useful technique is to track all the stages and people involved in a simple service or activity and to see how it could be simplified or better managed. It is also worth asking how the organisation could be designed around the user and the processes involved in meeting their needs rather than traditional specialist or professional boundaries.

Costing the project

Often new projects are under-costed. Sometimes this is because project developers believe that a cheap project will find it easier to attract funds or because the full cost of operating is either not known or not fully explored. Costing does require thorough work. Failing to identify costs or not including the full cost will usually create major problems for the project.

There are three different ways of dividing up the costs involved in a project:

◆ Costs that are recurring or non-recurring
◆ Costs that are directly related to the project, shared amongst other projects or are an indirect overhead
◆ Costs that are fixed or costs that are variable

Recurring and non-recurring costs

Recurring costs are costs that you expect to incur every year as part of the regular cycle of the project. The amount you spend may vary, but the heading will probably still be there every year.

Non-recurring costs are one-off costs. These are items which you do not expect to have to pay for every year. Projects often incur two kinds of non-recurring costs, capital and start-up costs.

Capital costs

Capital costs are expenditure on items which we do not expect to incur every year. Central and local government usually organise capital funding separately from annual revenue funding. Some capital items lose value over time. This is called depreciation. With capital items you need to calculate how many years you think the capital item will last for and divide this by the total cost. This gives a depreciation rate. For example, a car may cost £10,000. You estimate that it will probably last for five years. The car depreciates in value by £2,000 every year. If you are going to need a car permanently, you need to plan how you will build up a fund to meet this capital expenditure in five years. They also need repairing and eventual replacement. The purchase of capital items usually leads to an annual expenditure on running costs and maintenance. Examples of capital expenditure include buildings and major equipment purchase.

Start-up costs

Invariably a new project will incur some costs that are one-off items of expenditure because it is new. These include costs of the start-up phase and the costs involved in launching a new organisation. These costs should not be recurring ones and need to be budgeted for and accounted for separately. Start-up costs are often underestimated.

Costs that are directly related to the project, shared amongst other projects or are an indirect overhead

A project operating in or managed by an organisation can have three different types of costs:

Direct costs

These are the costs that are exclusively incurred by the project. If an environmental organisation set up a consultancy project, the costs of the project staff, their equipment, their administration and running costs could all be regarded as direct costs dedicated to the project. The organisation is only paying for these items because it has set up the project.

➲ Costing a project

A project operating in or managed by an organisation can have three different types of costs:

Direct costs
Costs which are only incurred because of the project. They are dedicated project costs.

Shared costs
Costs which the project shares with other projects and services.

Indirect costs
Costs not directly involved in the project but which are charged out to the project as an overhead cost or management charge.

Shared costs

Often projects share resources with other projects. It makes more economic sense for projects to share some costs. Examples include office space, administrative support and resources. The allocation of the total shared costs budget to each project can be established by measuring actual usage or by using an agreed formula based on the size of each project or by simply dividing the shared costs by the number of operating projects.

Indirect costs

Indirect costs are the costs of being part of the bigger organisation. They include shared organisational costs, central management costs and charges. This expenditure is not directly related to costs of the project.

Sometimes organisations describe the indirect costs (often together with the shared costs) as a management fee that it charges to a project's budget. In developing this approach to costing three things often happen:

◆ **The cost of the project is more than expected.** This can happen because the full costs have been identified for the first time. In the past, the full cost of operating a project may have been under estimated. A second reason might be that an organisation that fully costs its work is unlikely to have many 'slush funds' from where the real cost of operating can be subsidised.

◆ **Costs need justifying.** This process often causes a power shift in organisations as people start to question if the amount paid in indirect costs is a reasonable one. Does the central management really 'add value' to the project or is the project having to carry a top heavy bureaucracy?

◆ **The way costs are allocated can be arbitrary.** There are no strict rules about what is a direct, shared or indirect cost. For example, one agency ran five local projects. The agency coordinator felt that it was not right to regard all of her salary as an indirect cost. Instead, she reviewed her time and came up with a breakdown of 40% of her time being on the agency wide issues (an indirect cost), 30% of her time providing support and supervision to the projects (a shared cost) and 30% of her time split between two projects doing direct service delivery work (direct costs charged to the two projects).

Fixed or variable costs

Fixed costs are costs that you incur regardless of how busy you are. Variable costs relate directly to usage. For example a transport service will have to pay costs such as permanent staff wages, office rent and hire purchase on vehicles if it makes one journey or a hundred journeys a month as these costs are fixed. Costs such as fuel and sessional staff are variable items. The project incurs these costs in direct relation to how busy it gets.

The relationship between fixed and variable costs is particularly important in estimating a break-even point for projects which charge for their work. The break-even point is the point at which

---

● CASE STUDY

A youth development agency used this approach to cost out a telephone counselling project. It allocated all costs to one of the three headings:

Direct project costs	Shared costs	Indirect costs
Project worker's salary	30% of Info Officer salary	15% of Director's salary
Help line costs	20% of Agency office costs	15% of Central costs
Help line volunteer costs	15% of training budget	15% of Contingency costs
Help line publicity	15% of personnel budget	
Help line resources	15% of resources budget	
Start-up costs		
£29,000	£14,000	£11,000
Total cost: £54,000		

the project has enough business to have an income that is sufficient to cover its costs.

Current business thinking is to design organisations to be as flexible and as economic as possible by increasing the variable element through using sessional rather than permanent staff and buying in services from external suppliers when needed rather than having them permanently in the organisation. The long term effects and benefits of this strategy are not as yet clear. It could well be that increased use of variable items may be more costly and reduces morale within an organisation.

Understanding the financial structure of the project

As well as working out the likely costs of the projects and sources of expenditure thought needs to be given to the financial structure or the economy of the project. Four factors are important here:

+ The movement of money within the project
+ Patterns of cash flow
+ Pricing policies for projects which earn money
+ The need for sensible reserves and contingency

It is quite possible for a budget to balance but for the finances of the project still to be problematic. It is not just about the 'bottom line'. In setting up a project it is worth exploring the following potential issues:

Start-up costs subsidise the first year

Often the enthusiasm that there is for a new project means that funders can be quite generous at the start and provide money for the start-up. This is fine provided that the project does not rely upon start-up money in the first year to subsidise its running costs. One small project with a total income of £60,000 received a start-up budget of £12,000 in its first year. The start-up budget was often used for items which were of a recurring nature. This created serious financial problems in the second and third year.

Is the balance of costs right?

Is the balance between restricted and non-restricted income right? How do you make sure that all costs can be met? Can you justify the amounts paid in management and administration? There is no fixed rule as to what is an appropriate ratio between direct project costs and expenditure on organisational management. Some organisations aim to keep management costs to about 15 to 20% of the project's total costs. However, you can only make useful comparisons between projects if the same rules have been followed as to what is a direct cost, a shared cost and an indirect cost.

Are there any time lag problems?

Could a slow or a delayed start affect the project's income? It is usual for project expenditure to be high at the start of the project. Could this cause a cash flow problem?

How and when will we have to replace capital items? How long will our capital items really last for? When do we need to replace them? How can we set aside a fund to do this?

Will there be sufficient uncommitted working capital?

Is there sufficient flexibility in the budget? Will we be able to follow up opportunities and use our cash intelligently?

Staffing the project

In all projects so much of the project's success depends upon the quality and effectiveness of paid staff. Issues such as identifying the right skills needed, drawing up sound job descriptions and job roles and managing the recruitment process are critical. Often they are rushed or entered into as a bureaucratic chore rather than a critical task.

Skills needed

Skills change as the project develops and changes. Often commitment to the project's vision and values are seen as more important than getting the right skills. This is a hard issue. A commitment to or at the very least, an understanding of the project's vision and values in a small project will probably be an essential requirement for all staff. This needs to be looked at in perspective as no amount of commitment can compensate for a lack of appropriate skills.

Different skills for different times

A project needs to use the available skills of its staff and supporters throughout its life. The need for particular skills changes during particular phases of the project. The trick is to make sure that the project keeps encouraging the right people with the right skills to take a lead at a particular time and possibly to back off when their skills are not so central to project's current needs.

The skill mix needed in a project can change quite rapidly as the project moves into new phases. For example the skills needed in getting funds and setting up a service are different from ones needed to supervise, train and support a staff team.

In reality no project has the ability to turn on and turn off people and their skills as needed, but this sort of skill profiling does raise several issues about team development, staffing and project leadership.

One project was led by the person who had the big idea to set the project up. She was brilliant at communicating the vision, making deals with funders and getting things going. Somehow or other she assumed the position of project director. Once the project was up and running the project needed to create systems and develop services. She did not like to spend time on such mundane and bureaucratic

Project skills needs

In a review of two 3-year projects it was possible to identify how the skills of the project changed:

	Creative thinking			Organisational skills	Team leadership
Vision building		Analytical skills			
			Planning & design skills		

| Innovative phase | Testing feasibility | Building support for the project | Start up phase | First year |

			Legal / financial skills	Management skills
Influencing skills	Fundraising skills			
		Marketing skills		

activities. She preferred having ideas rather than turning them into long term workable solutions. It was not until she left the post that the project was able to recruit a new person to lead the project into its mainstream phase.

What would have happened if she had not left? Would the project have failed to develop? How could the project steering group have ensured that she recognised that her role had to change within the project? How could they have helped her to learn or develop new skills?

Skills audits, staff and committee appraisals, staff development and open discussion about strengths and weaknesses can help a project recognise and plan what skills it needs to take it on to its next phase.

The balance of skills needed within a project change over the project's lifespan. A useful exercise is to think about the type of skills needed now and how they will change over time. Some skills will remain constant, others will become more or less important at different times.

One project working with educational special needs experienced problems between the skills they really needed and the people they recruited. The treasurer of the management committee described her experience;

"The job adverts and job descriptions were not properly considered. What we needed in the staff team were people able to negotiate funds, organise an office, influence statutory partners and run training for our volunteer workers. The job advert, job description and the discussion at interview was all about our philosophy and practice in educational needs. We recruited two very talented case workers and then effectively asked them to become project managers. We needed them to set the project up and recruit volunteers who would do the core work. One person was able to work out what was needed and adapt to this. The other one hates doing anything but casework. He refuses to or is unable to do any project development work. It is our fault. We did not think clearly enough about what skills were needed".

Managing a fixed term project

It is useful to distinguish between a project in which the main funds are renewed every year and a project which is designed at the outset with a specific end date in mind. Most statutory authorities grant aid or contract for fixed time. Many projects exist on an annual cycle in which they apply every year for funds and hope that they will be successful. Increasingly, some organisations are now developing projects which have a fixed duration and do not envisage becoming permanent. These projects, given the uncertainty of annually renewable projects, need to think very carefully as to how they design and manage a time limited piece of work.

Broadly speaking there are three main approaches to planning time limited projects:

- **Ignore the time limit.** This high risk and somewhat reckless strategy has been adopted in several instances. Work on the basis that the project will be so good and so successful that funding will turn up to continue it and make it permanent.
- **Manage it with the end in mind.** Develop contingency plans and ideas in case the project does close, but manage it as if it is an ongoing entity. If funding does dry up then with time the project should be able to extricate itself.
- **Design the project with a clear end point.** Work on the basis that the project should be fixed term and will terminate. It could be replaced by permanent or new short term projects but its role is to stimulate and innovate change within a fixed period.

● CASE STUDY

A bad ending

Morton Leisure Development Project was a well planned and designed initiative. Its programme of health education and sports participation was well received, innovative and filled a much needed gap. It had secure funds for three years. Discussions of what would happen after the three years had been tactfully avoided.

Towards the end of the second year the project staff started to express concern about the long term future. A fund raising consultant was engaged to look at how the project could be funded in the long term. Approaches to possible funders were disappointing. They all recognised the useful and creative work of the project. Funders would like to find a way to help but there was little if any possibility of long term or core funding. The best on offer would be occasional bits of project funding.

In the third year the tone and style of the project changed. The project leader spent most of her time looking for alternative income to continue the project. Staff felt demoralised and worried about their future prospects. The level of work remained roughly the same, but the project lacked the spark that it once had. All energy and attention went into chasing after funding rather than developing the work.

Four months before the end of the project the staff and steering group realised that the chance of the project continuing after the three years was minimal. The best option would be to use some local authority underspend to delay the closure for a few months.

In the project's final six months the project faded away. Some staff left early. There was little enthusiasm and excitement about any of its events or activities. The impending closure loomed large.

Eighteen months on the project is forgotten about. People have a vague memory that something about health and sport was once run. Indeed there is now talk of creating a small project to do similar things, but called something different.

The former project leader makes the following observations of her experience:

◆ "We denied reality. From the outset no promise or indication was made that there would be or could be any long term funding. We ignored that and got carried away by our own enthusiasm. We organised our activities as if they would go on for ever. It would have been better if at the start we had asked ourselves what lasting difference five people with three years funding can make. We should have seen ourselves as pilots and developers rather than mainstream providers. We made the mistake of thinking like an organisation and not like a project. We wanted to be a permanent entity rather than focusing on creating change.

◆ "We should have worked towards the end. The hardest kind of fund raising is to go to someone and say 'our initial funding is about to run out. We will soon be out of work. We would like you to pick up the tab'. It is hardly a positive or enticing pitch. We should have put together a programme of spin off projects, new activities and other initiatives that could have grown out of the main project.

◆ "We should have ended on a high. It is hard to remember it now, but for the first two years the project was a huge success. It was dynamic and made a real impact locally. We lost it. We turned inwards and became focused on securing the non existent holy grail of permanent funding. Once we took our eye off the ball we lost it".

Badly managing a fixed term project or ignoring the reality until it is too late can cause several major problems:

Avoid sudden or badly planned withdrawal.

People with whom the project works or to whom its services are delivered continue to need and expect them. Sudden or badly planned withdrawal of the services can create massive problems for service users and communities. They are left high and dry. In some cases it might have been better not to have offered the service in the first place.

Staff uncertainty

Staff feel uncertain and insecure as they wait to hear if the project is to be extended or renewed for a further period. Their performance and enthusiasm wane. Many projects have been damaged through losing key people taking up more secure posts in the final phases of the project.

The project shifts from being focused on doing the work to being entirely focused on survival and funding. It falls into short term crisis management and diverts energy into scrabbling around for short term funding. No vision, direction or planning exists beyond that of getting funding.

In designing and planning effective fixed term projects the following ideas are important.

Sustainability

If the project is to run for two years what will be there in three years time? What will the project have changed? Some aspects of sustainability will be tangible such as buildings or resources, others might be intangible such as new skills learned or better practice being followed. An unsustainable project is one which leaves a gap when it stops working. People need it and expect it to be there. They cannot operate without it to support and manage them.

Focus on the end point

A useful technique is to develop a vision of how you would like things to be at the end of the project and then work backwards. This kind of scenario planning is a useful way of clarifying what kind of outcomes the project needs to achieve. The end of the project should be seen as the main target and all of the project's activities should lead up to that.

Develop a staff team that is geared around the end point. People applying for jobs with the project need to know that it will be of a fixed term duration. They will need support and practical help for them to find other work when the project closes. Secondments from other jobs or from outside of the organisation is one way of helping to overcome job insecurity.

End on a high point

Do not let the project fade out. Make sure that plans are made to record and disseminate its experiences. Make sure that the project's achievements will be identified, acknowledged and celebrated. This process needs to start early.

Developing an 'exit strategy'

Exit strategies are not easy. At times it is tempting to suggest that an exit strategy is a new concept used to make short term funding sound more intelligent and effective than it actually is. It implies that everything can be planned and managed to order. All the project has to do is set itself up, and then move into its prepared exit strategy. However, if projects are to be short term, serious thought does need to be given to what happens when the project, or its own sources of funding, cease.

Increasingly, exit strategies are requested by funders at the time when funding or project bids are being considered. At this stage it is difficult to prove

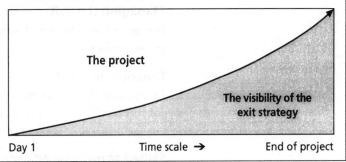

➔ Designing an exit strategy

The exit strategy should create something sustainable after the project has ended: new services, new projects or new skills. It should be in place from Day 1.

The project

The visibility of the exit strategy

Day 1   Time scale ➔   End of project

that the exit strategy will work. All you can show is that you have thought about it intelligently and have developed some plans. How the project closes down and what happens to its work are questions that need to be reviewed at key milestones throughout its life.

The following six examples are the kinds of strategies that can be used to make the project's work sustainable.

The project becomes permanent and self supporting

The project moves onto another stage. It is able to generate income from its activities or raise income from new sources.

The project is a one-off

No follow up is necessary as the project is planned to be unique. It can end without creating needs or leaving people expecting more.

The project is a demonstration project

The project must help others to learn from its experiences by documenting and sharing its experiences through training, reports, events and consultancy.

The project creates partners

The project identifies key groups and individuals who will be able to carry on its work after it has ceased. Their partners will need resources, support and early involvement in the project.

The project scales down its activities towards the end

The project only takes on work that it can complete within the time available. All work must therefore have clear completion deadlines.

Follow up projects and activities are created

The project sets up and secures resources for spin off projects and activities which should be able to operate independently when the project has ceased.

Managing the exit

For any of the above exit strategies to work, from the start the project must be:

Outcome focused

Everyone in the project must see the end point as being critical for the project. The project's outcomes should be identifiable, sustainable and not reliant on the project's staff.

Skilled at building alliances

Usually exit strategies depend on others. New people are needed to take the work on, to fund it, resource it and support it. The project must be skilled at transferring responsibility to the people who will take it on.

Skilled at managing change

The project needs to be focused on creating identifiable change. It has to help other people to support them in the exit strategy. It must be able to hand over its work, ideas and vision to others.

Firm with itself

The project needs to be disciplined. It must avoid taking on activities and commitments which it will not be around to see through or finish properly.

Getting the project organised

Once decisions have been made about the design, considerable work will be needed to get the project ready. All of these activities require hard work often to tight deadlines. In many respects what happens to the project is determined in the detail. Decisions made about legal structures, budgets and costs and personnel will have much more impact on the project's chance of success than time spent drafting vision statements.

Planning the project's start-up phase

The start-up phase needs to bring together all the different tasks that need performing and decisions that need to be made in a clear and logical way. The start-up plan needs to be produced in such a way that it:

- Sets out all the tasks and decisions involved in a clear and measurable way
- Matches the human and other resources available with the tasks
- Produces an easy to monitor plan that lets you note and record progress
- Highlights any departure from the plan at an early stage so that remedial action can be taken quickly to overcome delays, blocks or problems
- Produces key milestones for those involved in the project to work to

Quite often new projects are being set up against the clock. A deadline for the project to be working has been agreed and all the start-up activities must be carried out on schedule if the plan is to start on time. Examples of against the clock projects include when a funder has money to spend by a certain date (usually the end of the financial year) and the project must be operating by then or when there is a pressing political or other reason that determines when the project must be operating by. In such cases the start-up plan must balance expediency and realism. Individuals managing the start-up phase need to know that the tasks can be carried out in a sound manner. Failure to do so can lead to the project being bounced into commitments and promises that it struggles to meet or being set up to fail.

A simple planning framework is based around three key elements:

1. Starting at the end point and working backwards
2. Identifying key milestones towards the end points
3. Scheduling in and resourcing tasks and decisions to achieve each milestone.

Established project planning techniques

Project management as a branch of management studies has its main roots in the defence and engineering industries. Several techniques and systems have been drawn up to manage and plan complex projects. They all contain the following elements:

- Listing and estimating all the activities involved in a project
- Noting any dependent relationship between activities (e.g. activity x can only happen after activity y has been completed)
- Getting all the activities into a logical order
- Calculating the shortest time to get through all of the activities in a logical fashion

➲ A critical path plan

This is an example of using an established project management technique to plan the quickest time to agree a staff structure, recruit and appoint a worker for a new project. Each stage of the project has been identified, timed and had lead responsibility allocated to it. The stages are then put into a logical order. The thick line through it represents the 'critical path'. The critical path is the series of tasks that must be completed on schedule for the project to finish on time.

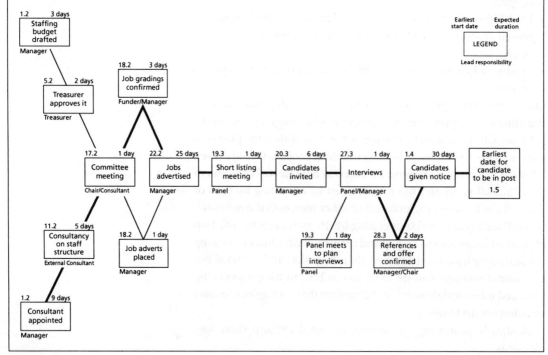

The three main techniques are:

Critical Path Model

A critical path is a method of calculating the total duration of all of the tasks involved in a project by estimating each task, linking it to others and working out the optimum route (the critical path) through from start to finish.

Programme Evaluation Review Technique (PERT)

PERT was developed in the 1950s by the United States Navy to schedule large projects. Similar to a critical path analysis a PERT chart (sometimes called a network diagram) sets out in graphic form the relationships between tasks and the overall likely duration.

Gantt chart

A Gantt chart (named after Henry L Gantt) sets out different tasks on a bar chart across a time scale. The strength of a Gantt chart is in its graphic representation and the ability to track progress quickly.

These techniques have a mixed reputation. They do provide a useful discipline, can help to get things in order and can identify

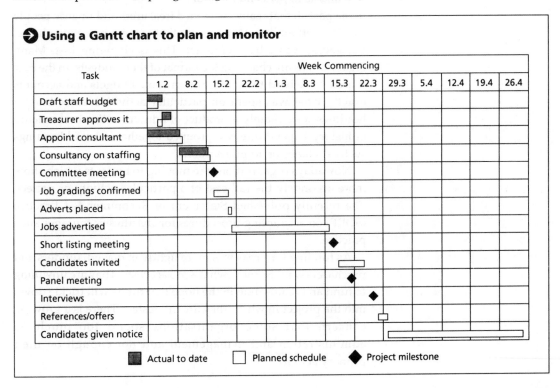

➡ Using a Gantt chart to plan and monitor

Task	Week Commencing												
	1.2	8.2	15.2	22.2	1.3	8.3	15.3	22.3	29.3	5.4	12.4	19.4	26.4
Draft staff budget	■												
Treasurer approves it	▫												
Appoint consultant	■■												
Consultancy on staffing		■■											
Committee meeting		◆											
Job gradings confirmed			▢										
Adverts placed			▫										
Jobs advertised				▢▢▢									
Short listing meeting							◆						
Candidates invited							▢▢						
Panel meeting								◆					
Interviews								◆					
References/offers									▫				
Candidates given notice									▢▢▢▢▢▢▢				

■ Actual to date   ▢ Planned schedule   ◆ Project milestone potential problems or delays. There is a tendency for them to become over complex and jargonistic. To use the technique properly all the details about time scales, deadlines and availability need to be available at the start of the project. There is also a tendency for planners to assume that everything works in a logical fashion.

All plans and all planning tools need to be active and flexible. They should not be regarded as shackles that tie down the project's development. Plans need to be reviewed and reshaped in the light of experience and developments. Effective and regular monitoring of the plan is vital.

Drawing up the project's first budget

As the project moves towards its launch, work will need to be given to its first budget. The first budget for a project must be able to do three things:

◆ Ensure that the project is able to function and has sufficient income to match likely expenditure
◆ Provide a control system for finance and also sufficient space for flexibility
◆ Ensure that the project has sufficient management information available to plan and monitor

In the past all that really concerned treasurers and finance people was the bottom line. Making sure that income met expenditure. Budgeting was a balancing act. This is changing fast. Many organisations are changing the format of their budgets. In the past it used to be hard to establish from some budgets and accounts exactly what was spent on particular activities, since budget headings were mainly a product of administrative convenience or history. Expenditure was grouped together in broad headings such as salaries or administration.

Nowadays organisations are moving to budgets which show more accurately the full cost of a particular activity or project. The recently published Statement of Recommended Practice (SORP) on accounting procedures for charities encourages such practice.

As funding for projects is more tightly managed, funders and purchasers want to know what a project costs. They are unwilling to fund an organisation in the hope that funds will trickle down into the project in which they are interested. There is a growing concern that some organisations spend too much on administration and management and not enough on their primary activity.

This means that projects need to be much clearer about the operating costs and the make up in the budget. Some organisations underestimate the cost of operating. This has led to impoverished organisations that can be criticised for 'always doing things on the cheap'.

About budgets

The budget is a statement of intent. Budgets must be related to objectives or strategy and not simply about balancing income and expenditure. The budget is the organisation's most deliberate statement of strategy and priorities.

Strategy not finance led

The budget should follow your strategy rather than dictate it. It is important that the budget setting exercise is firmly led by your plans and priorities.

Create flexibility

Good budgeting should allow some room for flexibility, new developments and opportunities.

Not fixed in stone

A useful practice is to periodically rebuild the budget as if you were starting again. This practice, called 'zero based budgeting', requires you to review all items and ensure that levels of spending are in line with your priorities. It stops the common practice of building all of the budget around past patterns rather than what you want to do in the future.

Start-up costs

Often in putting together a project the full cost of the start-up is underestimated. In the rush to get the project going key activities are under costed or overlooked. This checklist is a list of five areas of the most common start-up items:

People costs

The costs of job advertisement and selection are often high. Additional funds may be needed to include staff and volunteer training and temporary staff costs.

Premises costs

Careful budgeting is needed to plan for and control legal fees (such as the negotiation of leases), move in expenses and insurance costs. It is worth spending time researching the likely costs of bringing new accommodation up to a reasonable and safe standard as well as the costs of extra fittings, furniture and additional security. The costs of improving access to the premises need to be included in the project costs.

Operating costs

The purchase of operating equipment, such as computers, software, stationery and office materials must be included as well as the cost of any vehicle purchased.

Business costs

Two business costs need careful forecasting:

Slow start costs - Often new income generating projects have to build up a level of business. Their income will therefore be smaller in the first few months.

Cash flow costs - If a project spends proportionally more of its annual budget at the start of the year yet its income is received equally throughout the year then it will have a cash flow problem. The costs of meeting the cash flow gap (such as through a bank loan) need to be planned.

Launch costs

Costs involved in designing publicity materials and organising the project's launch need to planned and included.

Cash flow

It should be possible to sketch out the likely pattern of cash flow within the project for the first year. It is difficult to be exact about cash flow, but at this stage of a project's development any negative cash flow needs identifying. Three particular problems are common. First, that a project may not earn much income in its start-up phase because all of its activities are not up and running or take up is low. Secondly, that the costs of the project are likely to be greater at the start of the year yet income is spread evenly throughout the year. Thirdly, that the payment patterns of your main income sources are retrospective or prone to lateness. If there is likely to be a significant cash flow problem in the project it needs to be identified and resolved or the cost of managing cash flow built into the cost of the project.

Pricing policy

Increasingly projects are having to charge either the public or statutory purchasers for their services. Determining a pricing policy is a critical issue in the project's business plan. To do it effectively you must have sound and reliable information about what an activity costs. Costing should be an objective and rational exercise based on the relationship between different types of cost. Pricing is a much more tactical exercise. The following points need attention:

What is the break even point?

The break even point is the point at which your total income is equal to the total costs of the activity.

For example, The fixed costs of a training project are £300 per week, each trainee brings in a contract worth £45. The variable cost of each trainee such as equipment is £10. The break even point would be reached at nine trainees. Pricing strategies need to be based around achieving a viable break even point. When the break even point is reached the project has (at its current level of operation) covered its main fixed costs.

The project would reach a point were it could no longer take any more trainees without taking on more staff, expanding its base and possibly allowing the indirect costs to increase. In this example, we will assume that at around fourteen trainees the project hits breaking point. It needs more staff and other resources which are fixed costs. So it decides that in order to contine expanding (it could have chosen to say no...) its weekly fixed costs have to rise by £250 per week.

In this case the decision to increase fixed costs means that the project starts to make a loss. It needs to be confident that this is only a temporary loss and that soon they will be able to attract more trainees. Identifying and managing the break even and break point is tricky. Often projects have more than one or two break points. Some, such as the level of supervision or admin. support may not be easy to quantify as a number. Operating at or

➜ Setting the break even point

Number of trainees	Fixed cost	Variable cost	Total cost	Income	Balance (–loss)
12	300	120	420	540	120
11	300	110	410	495	85
10	300	100	400	450	50
(9)	300	90	390	405	(15)
8	300	80	380	360	–20
4	300	40	340	180	–160
2	300	20	320	90	–230
0	300	0	300	0	–300

➜ A new break even point

Number of trainees	Fixed cost	Variable cost	Total cost	Income	Balance (–loss)
17	550	170	720	765	45
(16)	550	160	710	720	(10)
15	550	150	700	675	–25
14	550	140	690	630	–60
(13)	300	130	430	585	(155)
12	300	120	420	540	120
11	300	110	410	495	85
10	300	100	400	450	50
9	300	90	390	405	15

beyond the break point can cause stress and is likely to reduce the quality and responsiveness of what you do.

The break even point is critical in projects dependent on a unit or fee based income. The break point is relevant in all projects that have to cope with demand and need to plan how best they can respond.

How does the market work?

Any feasibility study or business plan would need to have considered the price sensitivity of the market. What do similar and related providers charge? Who sets the price? What will the market pay for? How stable is it?

Avoid loss leaders

A loss leader is a deliberately low price set with the intention on enticing customers in. Once they are in you hope that they like it so much they will stay loyal to you as you raise your prices. Loss leaders are highly risky. Often all they do is create an expectation that the service is cheap.

How will the purchase be structured?

Can you reward purchasers for providing you with the security of a block purchase? Unit or spot based contracts often cost more. The organisation providing the service has to take a gamble that they might not reach their break even point. They build into their fee an element to cover the cost of this risk.

The need for sensible reserves and contingency

A controversial issue in the voluntary sector is to what level and for what purposes should charities build up reserves. On one hand, some people would argue that it is wrong to let money sit in a bank account when it could be being used for its intended purpose. On the other sound financial management would stress the need to cover problems, manage cash flow and emergencies and follow up opportunities. The Charity Commission has published a paper suggesting that reserves between two and twenty four months are reasonable. Each organisation needs to establish its own reserves policy based on the kind of risks which could occur and the need for effective planning. Thought needs to be given at the start of a project to ensuring such a fund can be built up.

Management information

At the start of the project decide what sort of financial monitoring and reporting system will be needed. This is a sensible thing to do in any organisation but is particularly important with a new project. The first year needs careful monitoring to check that the actual performance of the budget is in line with your original plans. If it starts to vary significantly then early action and decisions should be taken.

Drawing up an initial business plan

A business plan is an organisation 'setting out its stall'. It is a public statement of the overall aims, direction, management and financial plans for a project. Detailed advice on business planning is contained in my book **The Complete Guide to Business and Strategic Planning**. Several parts of the plan will have already been worked on in earlier stages of the project's development.

The main headings for a business plan for a new project are as follows:

- **A summary page.** A one page outline summarising the main points. This would be similar in content to the project outline.
- **Introduction and mission.** A brief introduction to the plan together with a short statement setting out the vision and values that are central to the project.
- **The background.** A short review of the history that led up to the creation of the project. This should also summarise the need for the project. If the project is part of or is sponsored by an existing organisation details of the organisation should be given.
- **A review.** A brief commentary on the main issues with which the project will deal. This should include a description of the need for the project, the gap that it will fill and the opportunities open to it.
- **Future trends.** A description of the main developments and trends that the project anticipates. Will demand for it rise? What political, organisational and social changes need to be taken into account? You will need to show evidence that the project has thought about likely changes to the environment in which it operates.
- **The strategy for the project.** A comprehensive outline of the main priorities for the project. What will its focus be? Specific, measured and timed objectives can be included to spell out the detail of what the project will do.

- **Implications.** What sort of organisation is needed to deliver the project? This would include a brief description of intended staffing, legal and management arrangements.
- **Financial Implications.** An outline description of the financial assumptions on which the project is based, the costs involved and estimated needed income.
- **Track record.** Some evidence that the people involved are able to deliver the project.

In a business plan for a new project the following six points are important:

- **Show that it has been thought through.** A good business plan shows that a project has been founded upon sensible assumptions and forecasts. It needs to set out the principles and conclusions of your thinking rather than detailed plans and budgets. Readers of the plan should be able to quickly understand the rationale and 'big idea' behind the project.
- **Honesty and openness.** A business plan needs to show that you have thought about potential risks or problems, analysed them and developed a strategy to deal with them. A business plan that attempts to 'gloss over' any risks or problems is unlikely to convince potential backers.
- **Don't predict what you don't know.** Many commercial business plans are inclined to be dominated by detailed attempts to forecast future cash flow, budgets and performance. Often this is a pointless exercise as the actual results rely on unknown circumstances and developments. In the first year of a project it may be possible to set out detailed plans. In the years that follow it is probably only feasible to cautiously estimate broad trends and developments.
- **Keep it active and short.** With business plans it seems that the longer the document, the more likely it is to be incoherent, imprecise and vague. It needs to be written in language which is focused on results. It has to be specific and clear. It is a working document that guides action rather than a policy paper of how we would like things to be.
- **It is more than a document.** All too often organisations and projects produce plans which are never referred to again. After initial circulation they are filed away and forgotten about. A good business plan needs to set out a strategy for a project in such a way that people in and around the project will understand it and use the plan as a guide. The plan must be measurable. Progress in achieving the plan must be monitored on a regular basis.

◆ **Focus on the main messages.** A useful exercise is to identify the main messages behind the plan and ensure that the plan highlights them. The plan can probably only deal with three to five main messages. The section on strategy and the executive summary of the plan must set out clearly the main issues leading up to the project and the overall direction behind the plan.

Recruiting the project's staff

It is interesting to note just how little time goes into recruiting staff in organisations compared to other decisions. Often key appointments are made on the basis of a forty minute interview whereas decisions of much less significance are researched, tested and debated. One manager commented that it amazed him that *"we spent a day interviewing and selecting candidates for the critical post of project leader. We actually spent much more time agreeing which contractors would equip and paint the project office".*

Most job descriptions are usually written to prevent disputes about whose job it is to do a particular task or to secure a pay grading. They are often long lists of possible tasks and responsibilities. They rarely convey a sense of what are the critical issues in a job or the balance of skills needed. In the main they are an administrative tool. To get away from this one American organisation now hires project managers on a one line job description - "do what ever is legally needed to make the project a success".

Increasingly, as part of good employment practice many organisations also produce a person specification setting out the essential and desirable skills and knowledge areas (sometimes called competencies) needed in the job. The job description and the person specification are important and do need careful attention.

In designing a job description the following features need to be clear:
◆ What responsibilities does the post holder have delegated to them?
◆ What resources does the post holder manage? What kinds of decision making power will they have?
◆ How will the post holder know that they are being successful?
◆ What are the key success factors for the job? What are the main priorities? What are the key processes involved in carrying out the job?
◆ What are the outputs and outcomes that the post holder needs to deliver?
◆ What will be expected of them? What skills are needed?

- What are the key relationships within the job?
- Who are the key people with whom the post holder must work effectively? This could include the importance of team work within the project.
- How might changes to the job occur?

You may consider building in a requirement that the post holder is committed to developing new skills and developing as the project changes.

Several organisations have experimented with producing a full job description for personnel and formal reasons and a working document such as a work plan to reflect job priorities at a given time. One agency sends out a one page list of the key priority areas for the applicant if they were to be appointed. It lists the core tasks needed rather than possible functions and responsibilities.

The primary method of recruitment, the job interview, is an incredibly flawed and faulty way of making an important decision. Interviews are often a very subjective process; they rely upon the skills of the interviewers to ask the right questions and to hold back from making subjective judgements. Some people would argue that all an interview really tells you is how good an individual can perform at a job interview. With this in mind the following points can help to strengthen the process:

Make it as objective a process as possible

Do all you can to remove the subjective elements of the process. Design all recruitment tests around a clear person specification that lists the essential knowledge and skills areas needed. Work out a format for interviews that will apply to all candidates. Make a list of the areas which you need to test or find out about and ensure that you have prepared questions that will reveal what you need to know.

Work with the panel

Make sure that all of the people involved in the recruitment and selection process have had some basic training in the processes and skills involved and also on issues concerning illegal direct and indirect discrimination in employment. All of the panel should apply the same criteria throughout the recruitment process.

Gather information and then make a judgement

See the process in two parts. The first part should be about gathering information to test candidates against the person specification. The second part should be about making judgements about their ability do the job as described. Often poor interviewers reverse this process. They make a snap judgement (often based on first impressions) and then spend the rest of the interview looking for evidence to support it.

Use other techniques

Other recruitment techniques can back up and support the interview. Commonly used techniques include presentations, practical tests and exercises, group discussion, psychological tests / profiles and written tests. All of them need careful planning and need to be related to the skills and experience that you have identified to do the job.

Don't rush the decision

Spend time checking that the job description and person specification really reflect what you want. Plan the interview carefully and be prepared to use second interviews or to re-advertise if you are not confident that you can make a good selection.

Planning the project's launch

The launch of the project should be an opportunity to develop the project's identity, create goodwill towards it and consolidate the networks of support that have developed during the start-up period.

In planning the launch think about how you will design and develop an appropriate and effective public identity for the project. This is often hard. Often you can be so close to a project that it is hard to think about it as if you were new to it. One law centre forgot to mention in its publicity material that it was both a free service and independent of local and central government. Both points were cornerstones of the centre's values. They were so obvious to the people in the project that they overlooked them.

There is also a danger in a new project of overselling it and promising too much. It is easy to set a project up as a panacea that will solve all known problems. If people believe that they will surely be quickly disappointed. In the launch stage it is sensible to indicate what the project cannot do as well as what it can do. One health project produced a simple leaflet to launch its services. On one side it said what it could do; on the other it listed things that it could not. The list of things that it could not do is as informative, if not more so, as the first list. It helps to develop a realistic expectation of what can and cannot be done.

In planning the launch it is worthwhile to work out the main messages which you want to get across. Try these messages out on people not connected to the project. Is the language that you are using appropriate? Is it riddled with technical language, initials and jargon that only insiders know? Does it convey the unique selling proposition of the project?

The launch should provide an occasion to consolidate goodwill towards the project by thanking people who have helped out in the start-up phase. It is also useful for making them feel part of the project as it goes mainstream.

8

The project's first year

The first year of a project is a critical time. In the first year of the project real life takes over. Objectives, goals and plans are determined by practice and circumstance rather than by how we would like to see things. Power and decisions shift from those who plan to those that do. Patterns and expectations are built up.

Keeping the vision central

Often in projects people assume that issues such as vision and values are clear to all involved. The assumption is held so strongly that no one takes the responsibility for checking that there is a central unity of purpose and ethos. In one relatively new agency thirteen staff, committee members and volunteers were asked to write down why they existed and what they believed was important about how the project operated. The statements were vastly different. For example, some thought that the aim of the project was to campaign against particular policies of the local authority. Others thought that its role was to develop long term partnerships and close relations with it. Many of the conflicts and uncertainties which the project experienced were identified as being linked to the lack of an agreed vision for the project rather than personality clashes. The person who set up the project and chaired the committee was surprised at how little unity there was within the project. She recognised an urgent need to redefine exactly what the project was about.

Management committees have a particularly crucial role in safeguarding and promoting the vision and direction of the project. Apart from their legal and constitutional obligations they can have a useful vantage point to observe the project and evaluate its development. The committee is a part of the organisation yet it is unlikely to be involved in the detailed day to day work. One popular way of describing its role is that it should focus on steering the direction and leave the rowing to the project staff.

The committee needs to periodically discuss the original vision that led to the project being set up. Useful prompts in doing this include:

- Is the vision still relevant?
- Are we making progress towards our vision?
- Is our strategy and planning clearly influenced by our vision?

CHAPTER SUMMARY

The importance of keeping the project focused on its long term vision

How the project's management committee can develop

The need for useful measurement and monitoring systems

Moving the project on from being new to mainstream

The case of the lost vision

The coordinator of an environmental project used his skills as a systems engineer to describe how his project lost its way. In a period of eighteen months the following series of events, causes and effects happened. Looking back he descibes the project's first eighteen months.

"When we launched we felt very positive. There was enormous support and goodwill for the project. Lots of people and agencies were keen to work with us. We did not see it at the time, but we became swamped by work and contacts.

"We took on far too much. We allowed ourselves to become involved in lots of different types of meetings and potential projects.

"We were soon being driven by being busy rather than by what we wanted to do. At first it felt good to be busy. But soon we were too busy to think. We became reactive. We only did things when it was the last minute and was urgent.

"We are now trying to get out of the crisis that we have created. We have to make sure that we are in the driving seat and are strategic about what work we take on.

"We need to develop good monitoring and evaluation systems to help us to question our work. We need to become skilled at saying 'no' and refusing to be bounced from idea to idea.

"Over the past six months we have been driven by urgency and activity rather than vision and direction. We must take action to restore it."

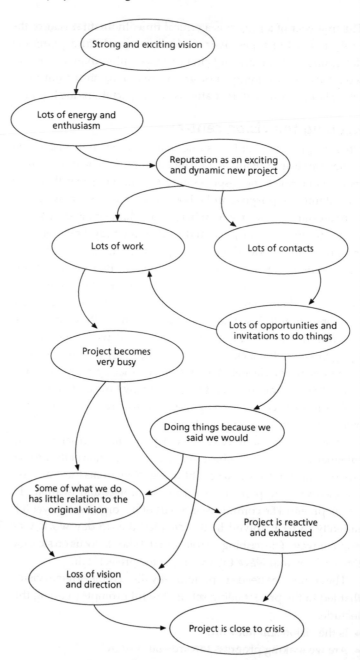

The vision should hold the project together and give it a sense of purpose. Often details and practicalities can weaken its significance. Pressure from funding bodies, new opportunities, organisational requirements and needs can all make the vision seem idealistic and remote. It has to be backed up with a strong and realistic strategy. But good strategy and sound management is not enough. Without a clear sense of vision or purpose the project will drift and achieve little.

It is very important that a project takes time to review progress and learn from the first year or so of operating. The review process needs to be built into to staff meetings, committees and planning sessions. It should provide the project staff with a chance to evaluate what they are doing, compare it to what the project was expected to do and plan the next stages.

How the committee's role changes

Projects that have management committees or boards to govern

Keeping the project under review

	Frequency of review	Questions
Visions and values – mission statement	Every few years or so –they should provide a long term purpose for the project	Are we still needed? What has changed? Do our vision and values guide all that we do?
The project's success criteria	Every few months	Are we likely to achieve our success criteria? What is working? What are the milestones towards success?
The project's strategy and direction	The strategy should be looked at regularly and reformed at least annually	Are we doing the right things? How can we make the best impact? What is happening in our environment? What should be our direction and priorities? What should stay the same and what should change?
The project's specific objectives and work plan	The specific plan should be agreed at least annually and monitored monthly	How do we implement our strategy? Are we on time and within budget? What else is happening? Are our outputs making an impact?
The project's critical success factors	The list of internal factors which have to work so that the project can be effective should be agreed at least annually and reviewed regularly	Where are the internal blocks within the project? What stops us being effective? How are we managing the critical success factors?

and oversee their work need to consider how the role of the committee changes during the first year or so. It is likely that in the period leading up to the project's establishment the committee members' individual and collective contribution will have been crucial in the early process. They will have nurtured the idea, developed the project plan and secured the resources to turn it into reality. As the project gets underway, the committee's role becomes less certain. Staff start to set the tone and pace of the project. Things need to happen too quickly for committee members to be fully informed of developments. They can very easily lose control. The committee can start to feel inactive or even redundant.

It is possible to look at how the committee develops as it moves through four stages:

Stage 1 The committee is highly active. It is involved with all of the day to day activity of the project. Its members carry out work and play a crucial role in getting the project established.	Stage 4 The committee steers. It is concerned with the long term direction of the project. It develops strategy evaluates work and ensures that the project keeps a vision.
Stage 2 The committee works with paid staff who take on an increasingly active role. The committee acts as a sounding board and supports the staff.	Stage 3 The committee acts as a rubber stamp. It approves the decisions taken by the staff. It has little direct influence on what happens. Its role is in the main a ceremonial one.

In stage one without the active contribution of the committee the project would not happen. Often in this stage there are no paid staff so the committee has to do the work.

Stage two can last for quite some time. The staff and committee find a way of communicating and keeping each other in touch. Over time the staff take on more responsibility and the committee's role becomes more 'backseat' or passive.

In stage three the committee only approves the decisions presented to it by the staff or makes decisions of major importance such as hiring and firings. It has little direct involvement in the project. Often the committee is composed of people who have been invited on to it to give the project credibility.

In stage four the committee is more concerned with directing rather than day to day management. It is concerned that the project has a strategy that will direct it towards its vision and that the project regularly evaluates its performance. Matters of operational detail are delegated to paid staff.

All of these stages have their positive and negative side. In stage one the contribution of volunteer committee members is crucial. More often than not they do the work. But, they need to give up these tasks as the project takes on staff. This is often a cause of conflict as committee members try to hang on to things they enjoy. In stage two the partnership can work well, provided there is a clear agreement about expectations, responsibilities and delegation. Often in this stage there is confusion as to what can be decided by the staff and what they need to take to the committee. It is not at all unusual to find committees having long debates on minor items of expenditure while major decisions relating to the project's long term future go through without discussion. Many management committees operate at stage three. They claim to have an arm's length relationship to the project and insist that it is not their role to meddle in the day to day workings. They are there to lend authority, support and guidance when needed, although they can often become remote and know little about what is really happening. They are too out of touch to operate good governance. In stage four, the committee is often able to help the project staff see the bigger picture, by encouraging evaluation, measuring progress and keeping the project in line with its vision. Doing this well requires some considerable skill, good information and a 'feel' for the style and culture of the project. Often as a committee moves through these stages some members fall away or are reluctant to move on. Several projects have had to find ways of managing round their committee.

The following seven points are possible strategies in helping committees to move on and develop alongside the project.

Encourage committee review sessions

Encourage the committee to review at least annually its performance and role. In one project the management board reviews its effectiveness every four months at the end of its business meeting. They work through five questions:

- What have we as a committee added to the project?
- What do we need to do more of?
- What do we need to do less of?
- What are the main issues which we need to focus on?
- Are we keeping to our business plan?

Run a skills audit

Encourage the committee to review its membership and skills regularly. Several organisations now use skills audits to encourage committees to review their membership and identify any gaps. They usually work by the committee identifying what skills and knowledge basis are needed to effectively govern the organisation and then to identify gaps in the committee's membership.

Stress responsibilities

Be clear what is expected of committee members. Charitable law places an obligation on trustees always to act in the best interest

● CASE STUDY

Overstaying your welcome

Anyone who knew Pengor Arts Centre would agree that Martin had been central to setting it up. It was his idea. He had built support for it, found the building and navigated the project through complicated planning applications and funding bids. He had chaired the committee from the start, and had taken on a whole host of other roles from spokesman to caretaker. In the three months between the centre opening and the new Director starting he had acted as unpaid Director as well. At times it had looked as if the centre would not get off the ground. It was a tribute to Martin's vision and energy over three years that it had.

Sam, the new Director, found the centre in good shape. She and Martin worked well together. He had plenty of ideas and contacts, she had lots of the necessary managerial and financial skills. She decided to spend the first few months getting the centre organised. Several things such as proper budget systems and basic health and safety issues had been neglected in the rush to get it going.

In retrospect tensions between Sam and Martin were obvious at the second management board meeting. She presented two papers. The first set out a new budget. The current budget had unrealistic income predictions. Savings would have to be made. Some projects may have to be delayed. The second paper called for a reduced programme of events. There was a danger, she argued, of doing too many things badly. It was better to do a few things effectively in the first year and then build up. Martin hurried the discussion through. Although the papers were agreed he showed no enthusiasm for them.

The Treasurer of the committee met Sam after seven months in the job. She said that the 'honeymoon period was well and truly over'. When pressed she explained that Martin carried on regardless. Every week he had at least three ideas about what the centre could do. He regularly made commitments on the centre's behalf without telling Sam. He ignored the perilous financial situation by arguing that money always turned up for good ideas. Sam respected Martin a great deal. She just felt stifled by him.

The Treasurer talked to Martin about the situation. He admitted to feeling frustrated. He genuinely supported and understood what Sam was doing. But it just was not fun any more! Setting it up and getting it going had been exciting. Running it was not.

Martin thought about his position. In January he shocked everyone by resigning from the committee. He could not see any way of scaling down his involvement. He did not want to be only involved on the fringes of the centre. He realised that it was time for him to move on.

It was with a genuine feeling of regret that the committee accepted Martin's decision. Sam did feel a sense of loss, but felt that she could now do the things she was paid for without being blocked.

Martin's resignation raised several issues about the role of the founder in a project:

◆ Is there a point in the project's development when the founder or original visionary needs to allow others to take over? Are they so central to everything that they could block other people's development and growth?

◆ Are some people better at setting projects up and being innovative than at managing projects?

◆ What kind of structures and processes are needed in a project to review the kind of management needed at a given time? How do you stop relationships breaking down between people? How do you review different contributions that people can make?

Six months later Martin is very busy launching a youth project. He is full of energy and enthusiasm for it. But this time he plans to start it, hand it over and then move on.

of the charity. This places a specific expectation that committee members are responsible for putting the needs and interests of the organisation first (something with which co-opted members often find it hard to come to terms).

Agree expectations

Several organisations produce a job description for the committee setting out minimum requirements and obligations. Others agree how much time committee members should expect to have to give each month to the project. If committee members regularly go over this time it probably means that they are meeting too much, that they are too involved in day to day matters or that the project is in crisis.

Manage information

Regularly review the information needs of the committee. Often committees get too much or too little information. They are swamped with reports and papers or alternatively they are kept in the dark. The flow of information between the staff and committee needs to be negotiated and agreed. The information that the committee needs to keep itself informed, exercise its responsibilities and contribute to the project's long term direction must be identified.

Train and support committee members

In several projects committee members are very much in touch in the early days of the project, but lose touch with new developments. Often so much is happening in a particular organisation, field or sector that it is very hard to keep up to date. One committee member described how she realised that she was out of touch with her project.

"We are involved in special needs housing. I am an accountant so I was lined up to chair the finance sub committee. Housing finance in general and special needs finance in particular changes rapidly. Often in discussions I realised that I was out of date. I was concerned that my slowness could block the project's development. To keep up to date with developments would be a full time job. I do not need to know and indeed probably should not know the detail. That's what we have a finance officer for. What I do need to know is the general picture and the right questions to ask. We now have a training budget for the committee. We use it for attending courses and briefings externally and for running three in house committee briefings a year."

Encourage the committee to have a 'helicopter vision'

Effective committees can make a unique contribution to a project. They should understand the project's purpose and values. Yet they are not part of it on a day to day or week to week basis. They should be able to operate a helicopter vision by 'rising above the day to day detail and helping the project to take a broader view of what is happening'. They need to help the project by ensuring that the direction is not lost and occasionally helping the project stand back from the activity and take a fresh look at itself.

Measuring up

Performance indicators, impact and outcome measures and terms such as value added are all part of new management language that can dominate much of our thinking and discussion about project planning, resourcing and management. Measurement is a vital part of management. In some cases attempts to design or impose measurement systems on projects have been troublesome. Two things can go wrong:

We only bother to measure and monitor because funders require it

Most funders now insist that regular information is provided by projects as a way of monitoring progress and ensuring that their investment is properly used. Much of the language of measurement is simplistic, finance driven and can ignore some of the complexity of what you do. Often new projects are required to complete detailed monitoring forms that only focus on the things that are easy to measure. The volume appears to be more important than the effectiveness of what you do. This needs challenging. Funders need to be shown much more interesting measures. Projects need to be able to suggest their own measures rather than simply responding to what funders demand.

Wasting time measuring things that are not important

There is a real danger of over measurement. Once we start identifying things which can be counted it is difficult to stop. It is sensible to identify a few useful measures which give a feel of what the project is doing and achieving. Be careful not to over measure. Too much information will frustrate those who have to collect it and confuse those who have to interpret it.

In designing measurement systems it is worth considering the following points:

◆ Balance output and outcome measures.

- Quantitative measures are not usually enough.
- Collecting data about throughput, volume and output is important, but it rarely gives a full feel of how effective the project is or of the quality of the work.
- A range of measures of both output and outcome should be used.

Outcome measures are usually harder to collect

It often takes time for a project to have an impact. Sometimes an effective outcome is prevention (for example an early intervention might be the thing that stops a crisis). The measurement process of outcomes cannot always be reduced to a set of numbers. You often have to make an informed judgement about the effect of the project.

Keep the monitoring system simple

Monitoring systems will fail if they generate unnecessary paperwork and control systems. Try to design the monitoring system around the organisational and management systems that already exist. Diaries, booking systems and case records can all be used as the basis of a system to collect information.

Think about how the information will be interpreted

Numbers on their own can easily be misread or misinterpreted. This is particularly true when information is looked at by people who are not directly involved in the day to day work of the project such as funders or management committee members. To make sense of the figures which show that one community worker worked with six groups and that another worked with eleven groups in a month needs some knowledge of the context, purpose and practice of community work. The figures on their own are meaningless. You need to build around the numbers a simple commentary which indicates targets, good practice and relevant quality standards. You also need to be able to explain any problem which could have held back performance.

Moving the project on

The project's journey from being a new entity to its mainstream phase needs careful thought. Often projects are launched with tremendous enthusiasm and confidence. There is a lot of energy and willingness to experiment. But at some stage it needs to move on. It needs to establish a pattern of work that is sustainable and realistic.

Output measures

- Volume
- Numbers taking part
- Income raised
- Activities
- Services delivered

Outcome measures

- Did the output create change?
- Did the benefits last?
- What impact are we making?
- How are we affecting needs?
- What is happening as a result of our work?

A health project experienced considerable 'growing pains' in moving from being a new project to being a mainstream one. Its first two years had been full of innovation and experimentation. It developed a series of health programmes that were very popular and broke new ground. A great deal of staff time went into programme development and design. Towards the end of the second year negotiations started with local health and social care authorities for two to three year service contracts. The purchasing authorities were very keen on the project, but 'needed to see numbers'. They wanted to have significantly more programmes with a minimum of ten participants. In the first two years the project had rarely ever ran the same programme twice. It constantly redesigned, evaluated and developed its product. It took a considerable effort of will to move from developing the prototype to moving into service production. One of the project workers talked about how:

"We wanted to keep improving the prototype, but really that was unrealistic. We had to find a way of delivering the programme in a way that was cost effective and efficient. We had to move the project on. We did not want to move away from our research and design activities. We were inclined to be perfectionists. But the reality was that we had to find a way of making the programme viable and to show that it could be delivered".

In moving the project on the following eight issues need planning and managing:

The project needs to consolidate

After its start-up phase a project needs to change pace. It needs to develop effective ways of organising its work and maintaining relationships internally and externally. Project staff should spend some time developing processes and systems that enable and support the project's work. Teams and effective committees need training and support to help them to work well. External partners, backers and contacts need to be worked with to sustain and develop their good will towards the project. Often people resist consolidation. Doing new things, making new plans and developing new relations often seems much more exciting.

Identify and build upon early successes

Success creates more success. All too often in not-for-profit organisations successes are ignored and not acknowledged. One experienced public sector worker described how she only ever found out about her good work and the successes that she had contributed to at her leaving party. In projects it is useful to look for and celebrate early examples of the project making a successful impact. This can help to encourage other successes, it can create a positive atmosphere and can make people feel that their past and current contribution worthwhile.

Watch out for complacency

It is very easy to become complacent once a project has started working. It is tempting to fall into routines, stop thinking and start driving on 'automatic pilot'. The project does things because 'we have always done it that way'. Regular evaluation sessions, contact with outside agencies, a commitment to learning, the involvement of new people and a constant curiosity can overcome complacency.

Stopping the project being bounced into other things

Often in a project's first year new opportunities emerge or circumstances change. These opportunities and changes have to be balanced against the project's agreed strategy and plan.

Managing changes to the plan is difficult

A refusal to think about change by rigidly sticking to the original idea will probably be perilous, whilst continually adjusting and altering the project throughout this phase will probably mean that the project will lose its cohesion, identity and original vision and values. If changes are to be made then they should be made in an explicit way by rewriting the original project strategy and success criteria rather than incorporating them by absorption.

Think carefully about further growth

If a project is developing well it is tempting to think about expansion beyond its original base. Projects may choose to expand in size, in geography or in scope. Growth can be very exciting. But badly planned it can also cause problems. It can

---

> ### ➜ Ten reasons to close a project down
>
> ❶ It has achieved its purpose/mission
>
> ❷ Other people do the same thing consistently better
>
> ❸ The project's output is not worth the input
>
> ❹ The original assumptions/needs and driving forces behind the project have changed significantly
>
> ❺ The only purpose served by continuing would be to continue to exist as an organisation
>
> ❻ The work of the project is persistently dogged by internal conflicts and disputes that stop work from being done
>
> ❼ It has fundamentally lost the confidence of its users and backers
>
> ❽ It is no longer financially viable or solvent
>
> ❾ The project's resources could be used to much greater effect elsewhere
>
> ❿ Any of the above plus the lack of a critical mass of people inside and outside the project committed to turning it round.

133

lead to uneven development, put strain on the organisation, pull resources out of the existing activities and reduce the sharpness of the project's original focus. Growth needs to be thought through. What is the project's optimum size (i.e. when it is able to do what it wants to do most effectively)? Can the lessons and circumstances of one successful project be replicated into others?

Should the project aim to become permanent?

Often fixed term projects see becoming a permanent organisation as something to aspire to. In many ways this is understandable. But, some projects are successful because they are not permanent. They are focused and build up an energy and focus because their time is limited. Such success factors are often difficult to transfer into a permanent organisation. Sometimes, it is more effective to spend time early in the project's life developing strategies that will enable the project's work to be carried on or taken up by others on a more longer term basis rather than the project spending it's effort chasing long term funding.

Think about the project's life cycle

Projects seem to have a certain ecology. They can develop and grow fast, they reach a peak and then a plateau. Unless something changes (or the project closes) the project can slowly or quickly drift into decline. The original energy and direction that set it up can easily (and sometimes quickly) drift away. Regular reviews, creative thinking, good strategic management can help to monitor where you are on the project's life cycle. They help to plan for and think about what comes next.

Useful publications

Accidental Empires
Cringely / Viking
The brilliantly written story of how the personal computer industry was created 'more or less by accident by amateurs who for the most part still are'
ISBN 0 670 84561 2

Across The Geographical Divide
Stan and Mari Thekaekara
Centre For Innovation in Voluntary Action
A fascinating report by two Indian community workers of their visit to UK anti poverty projects
ISBN 1 873860 78 1

Building on Innovation
Norton
Joseph Rowntree Foundation
Report of a study into how successful projects can be replicated
ISBN 1 873860 87 0

Costing for Contracts
Callaghan
Directory of Social Change
A useful guide to costing services and projects
ISBN 0 907164 81 1

Innovation and Entrepreneurship
Drucker / Pan Business Books
A look at how businesses can encourage innovation
ISBN 0 330 29465 2

Project Leadership
Briner, Geddes & Hastings / Gower
A practical guide to creating project teams and developing systems for project based organisations
ISBN 0 556 02794 1

Superteams
Hastings, Bixby & Chaudhry-Lawton / Fontana
An interesting look at how effective teams are developed and encouraged
ISBN 0 00 637049 7

The Complete Guide to Business & Strategic Planning
Lawrie
Directory of Social Change
A detailed guide to putting together a business and strategic plan for voluntary organisations
ISBN 1 873860 61 7

The Creative Manager
Evans & Russell / Unwin Books
A guide to how managers can develop their own problem solving and creative skills
ISBN 0 04 440604 5

The Fifth Discipline Field book
Senge, Ross, Smith, Roberts & Kleiner
Nicholas Brealey Publishing
A practical introduction to the development of the idea of a 'learning organisation'
ISBN 1 85788 060 9

The Once and Future Pioneers
Osborne
Joseph Rowntree Foundation
Research report on the extent of innovation within the voluntary organisations
ISBN 1 85 449146 6

Computer software and information

Idea Fisher
Idea Fisher Systems
A creative thinking tool - useful for encouraging brainstorming and lateral thinking.

Inspiration
Inspirations Software
A very practical and visual idea development tool for developing and presenting ideas and plans.

Microsoft Project
Microsoft
A programme designed to develop and run traditional project planning tools such as critical path and Gantt charts. A complex tool for big projects.

MacProject
Claris
A critical path planning tool for Macintosh users.

The Institute For Social Inventions
The institute operates through an internet page:
http://www.newciv.org/worldtrans

The Institute acts as a clearing house for innovative social ideas. It awards an annual prize for the most interesting ideas.